revenge
of the
paste eaters

(memoirs of a misfit)

CHERYL PECK

NEW YORK   BOSTON

5 Spot
Time Warner Book Group
1271 Avenue of the Americas, New York, NY 10020
Visit our Web site at www.5-spot.com.

Printed in the United States of America

First Edition: October 2005

10 9 8 7 6 5 4 3 2 1

Library of Congress Cataloging-in-Publication Data

Peck, Cheryl.
   Revenge of the paste eaters : memoirs of a misfit / Cheryl Peck.
   p. cm.
   ISBN 0-446-69373-1
   1. Peck, Cheryl—Anecdotes. 2. Lesbians—Michigan—
Anecdotes. 3. Feminists—Michigan—Anecdotes. 4. Michigan—
Biography—Anecdotes. I. Title.
   CT275.P52155A3 2005
   306.76'63'00973—dc22

                                                2005010470

Book design and text composition by Nancy Singer Olaguera, ISPN
Cover design by Brigid Pearson

This book is dedicated to my first editor,
my computer tech, head cheerleader,
frequently consulted critic, sales rep, and
surrogate daughter: Ranee, you have no idea
how relieved we are to have you still among us.

acknowledgments

i would like to thank my friends, who have stood behind me, my partner, who has stood beside me, and my family, over whose quiet reputations I have walked, not always gently, to tell my stories.

Recently I attended my first-ever writers conference, where I learned how incredibly difficult it can be to get an editor to call you back or even discuss what is happening with your manuscript, so I would particularly like to thank my editor, Amy Einhorn, for her patience, her sense of humor, and her availability. She has been a joy to work with. And I send a big hug also for Keri and Jim, and everyone else at Warner.

I would also like to take a moment to thank Daryla for our new tile floor (they seem to go hand in hand, new book project, new flooring project) and my friend Bob, my own personal media escort. And I would like to thank Annie, of course, just for being, and all of those dedicated bookstore owners everywhere, who struggle to keep the written word available and alive.

contents

introduction

when we were kids my dad gave us the most wonderful gift any of us have ever received—the box that the family's new freezer came in. We lived in our box for weeks. We lived in the box in the front yard; we lived in the box in the back yard. We hauled the box down into the gravel pit behind our house and lived there for a while. We had essentially discovered the joy of owning a travel home. Unfortunately, it rained on our box one day and our most wonderful gift disintegrated into a sticky, sloppy mess. None of us have looked at Winnebagos quite the same since.

While we still had the box, however, we were anything but contented, cooperative little homemakers. It occurred to each of the three of us—the Wee One, the UnWee, and me, the Least Wee—that we would have considerably more room and greater creative freedom inside our box if one of us were, in fact, the sole occupant. Small wars broke out. A lot of secretive stalking went on. The box traveled all over the back yard from one enemy camp to the next. Various complaints and accusations were filed with higher authorities until our mother, ever the Solomon of our lives, decreed that if any more bickering reached her ears, she would organize a bonfire on the spot. This at least united us against our mother.

What I remember is that my little sisters banded together and plotted against me. They were an unassailable union, speaking their own private language, understanding each other often without words . . . In a few short years I had gone from being the firstborn to the left-out, and much of my life at that time I spent wandering the gravel pit and feeling sorry for myself.

Curiously, neither one of my sisters remembers this bond. At best, they tolerated each other. They are, in fact, no different from any other two random people a year and a half apart in age who happened to be thrown into the same family. They were not—and are not—enemies, by any means, and they are sisters; but the unbreakable bond between them, it turns out, was my own family fiction.

The stories in this book are very much like that. People always ask me, "Is that story true?" and there is no real answer for that question. Parts of every story are true. Parts of every story were enhanced, or exaggerated, or "fine-tuned" to make it a better story, and probably parts of every story are just misremembered. Family fiction. If you were to ask any other member of my family, "What exactly happened when . . . ?" you might get a completely different answer from the one I give you here. Their version might be every bit as true for them as mine is for me. That's just the nature of stories, and the nature of families.

When I first published *Fat Girls and Lawn Chairs* I was prepared to become both rich and famous. Cruising through the mansions on Bronson Boulevard, I thought to myself, *I may have a house like this someday.* I planned my premature retirement from my day job. I imagined what I might say to my adoring audience from the *Oprah* show. All of that turned out to be yet another example of enhanced fiction, but I did have a wonderful time spending the volumes of money I would make as a published author, and composing acceptance speeches for the many awards that would be bestowed upon me.

I have since returned to earth.

You don't have to have read *Fat Girls and Lawn Chairs* to follow this book. Many of the same characters reappear here—family members, of course, my Beloved, her daughter the Girlchild, our friends Rae, Annie, and Bob. In fact, this is a sort of "inquiring minds want to know" introduction that answers the most common questions people ask me: How is your dad? How does your family feel about your writing about them? How is Babycakes? Why do you have such cutesy names for your family members, friends, etc.? Is she your "Beloved"?

helpful things to know

I am the oldest of five children, three girls and two boys. All of the girls are older than all of the boys. The youngest boy is twelve years younger than I am, which means he was in kindergarten when I was a senior in high school. His childhood exploits are not well documented here. My mom was a stay-at-home mom until my baby brother was born, and shortly after that she went to work as a secretary for a shoe company and then for the state of Michigan. My father drove a fuel oil delivery truck when I was a child, then for a while he delivered groceries, and eventually he also went to work for the state, as a groundskeeper.

how is my dad?

I love my dad, but he can be stubborn. For something like fourteen years he dated his lady friend and enjoyed her company, but refused to marry her because he felt he had historically spent "too much of my married life out in the garage." (This refers to his preferred method of dealing with conflict—avoidance.) She nursed him through spinal meningitis and the valve job his heart required as a result of the meningitis, but when she caught him, six weeks out of the hospital, trying to tote around his breadmaker (he had a five-pound weight-lifting restriction) she washed her hands of him and followed her life dream to return to her family in Alabama. They dated long-distance for two years, and then, as a result of the medications he takes to manage his new valves, he suffered several strokes. The strokes effectively ended the independence he had savored for so long and brought him face-to-face with a difficult decision: should he move in with one of his children, or move to Alabama?

We struggled with this question: it appears he did not.

So at the age of seventy-six, my father, who never has voluntarily left the state of Michigan, moved to Alabama, where he has now lived for two years. From time to time, just to annoy his eldest daughter, he refers to his partner as "Oh, that woman who lives here." (His stroke affected areas of speech and memory, thus rendering a man who has never found verbal communication easy just plain helpless sometimes. He lives with her, but he has trouble remembering her name.) Because it can be difficult (and can change from one day to the next) to determine exactly what he does want, there is now a steady stream of adult Peck children running up and down I-65, plumbing his mind and listening for echoes of homesickness or mention of distress over the fact that the only saint he has ever known does not in fact have a garage where he can avoid her. He is older. His life is more limited. He seems happy.

how does my family feel about my writing about them?

Conflicted. Having grown up with the constant clatter of a typewriter in the room next door, I think they are pleased and proud that I seem, at this late date, to be achieving my life dream. Anyone's family would be delighted to discover that one of their members has begun receiving irregular and unexpected checks they never received before. I think my being published after writing a book about them has affected them much like discovering that I'm a lesbian: it's not what they would have planned for me, but it explains so much, and there is always the remote chance it will eventually make me a happier person—and God knows it beats all that existential angst I so perfected in high school.

On the other hand, I think there is a kind of helplessness one feels when someone who sees you far differently than you see yourself gives their "wrong" view of you the peculiar authority that the written word acquires. And there has been precious little in the values and world-view we were raised with that would prepare us to be going about our normal lives and have someone walk up to us, point, and say, "I *know you—you're the Wee One.*" Privacy is always an issue.

Before *Fat Girls* was published we would gather at family events and trade stories back and forth about our childhood, and when I had finished one of mine my siblings would look at me like I had grown antlers and demand, "Where *were* you when we were kids? That's not how that happened, so-and-so wasn't even there, and those are two completely separate events . . ." Since the book has been published, they now say to each other, "You'll have to ask Cheryl—she's the one who remembers all of that stuff . . ." The credibility of my memory has not changed. My appreciation for the power of the written word has.

how is babycakes?

Twelve years old and as agile and self-satisfied as ever. He still plays the odd game of golf, maintains a fine collection of busyballs, and relentlessly hunts bugs, shadows, and wild hairs. He takes his work as feline alarm clock and bathroom attendant very seriously. Since Mommy got a digital camera, he has been trying his hand as male model.

and is this your "beloved"?

Yes. Still. Eight years and counting. See "How Does My Family Feel . . ." She is a woman who enjoys intimate sharing and public privacy. I am a person who would tell the person sitting next to me on the bus all about my love life. But I am not always good about clueing in the people who live with me every day. I was an unpublished writer when she met me. I don't suppose either one of us imagined that would ever change—or how it might affect us, if it did.

revenge of the paste eaters

in our fifth grade art class there were two acknowledged artists, Louisa McFarland and Samantha Serene.
Billy Stewart was clever, but his artwork was more
inventive than fundamentally skilled. We knew what we
could do, and we could have done what Billy Stewart
did, if only we had thought of it: when Samantha or
Louisa drew a picture of a dog, we could not only distin-
guish which species of four-legged animal they drew, we
could identify the *breed*. Billy Stewart would have made
us see that what he drew was a dog as well, but he would
have done something like incorporating the letters into
the shape. Trick art. We were not looking for creativity
in our fifth grade art class. We were looking for a repre-
sentation that required more dexterity and deeper vision
than the rest of us had. We were literal critics and we
were looking for literal art.

Off somewhere in the distance the Adults—that vast,
amorphous collection of order-giving people taller than
we were—were Doing Something, but I have long since
forgotten what. Whatever it was, they wanted everyone
to know about it, and to make that happen they needed
posters. Lots and lots of colorful, attention-grabbing
posters. Some bright Adult must have turned to others of

his kind and said, "Let's get kids to do it—everybody loves kid art, and they'll work dirt cheap." And the poster contest was born.

"You could win prizes," our teacher told us as she wrote the pertinent poster information on the blackboard. She passed out sheets of construction paper while continuing, "The first prize is ten dollars. You just have to make sure that the words on the blackboard appear somewhere on your poster."

We studied the board critically. Some of us squinted with one eye and held up certain colors against the backdrop of the blackboard, rocking the sheets to the right or left while we conjured up our designs. Others twisted our hair around our fingers or chewed our erasers while deep in thought. We had plans for that ten-dollar grand prize, each and every one of us. *I'm going to spend mine on bubblegum,* one hopeful would announce, while another practiced looking solemn and wise and prematurely rich.

"Don't eat the paste, Cheryl," the teacher warned me as she set the jar on my desk. Our paste was white and came in quart jars like mayonnaise, and when it dried out it turned that same translucent color on the edges of the glass. I loved paste. I don't recall that it had much taste. Vegetarian grease, perhaps, if there were such a thing, would have tasted like grade school paste. No one ate it for the taste: we ate it for the smell, which was some distant member of the mint family—wintergreen, perhaps—and those of us who ate paste ate it as if eating enough of it would make it taste the way it smelled.

Everyone in the class made a poster. Some of us used parts of those lacy paper napkins, while the design purists utilized nothing but colored construction paper. Some of us used big, bold designs, and some of us preferred to gather our art tidily down in one corner of our poster and let the space draw the viewer's attention to it. Some of us would wander past Louisa McFarland's or Samantha Serene's desks and then return to our own projects with a growing sense of despair. Life was not fair. It was yet another grown-up trick of the sort they seemed especially fond, making all of us believe we had a fair chance, and then always—*always*—rewarding the same old winners.

I believe my poster featured a sailboat, but I can't say that with any certainty. I made it. I admired it. I determined it to be the very best of all of the posters I had seen, and then I turned it in.

Minutes passed.

No one came along to give me the grand prize, and then someone distracted me, and I probably never would have thought about that poster again.

Except I won.

My poster won the grand prize.

I was still sitting at my desk, thinking, *What poster?* when the teacher gave me an envelope with a ten-dollar bill in it and everyone in the class applauded for me. I might have enjoyed my moment of artistic glory more if I could have remembered the poster, but it was attention and I sucked up attention like a damp sponge.

I won, and I had a ten-dollar bill in my pocket to prove it.

I had pretty much forgotten it all over again ten min-·utes later.

Ten minutes later was when Louisa McFarland walked up to me and said, "Congratulations on winning the poster contest."

I nodded politely. Louisa McFarland did not talk to me all that often. Not many of my classmates did. I was a good student who got along well with teachers, but I had yet to strike that delicate balance of tact and discretion so necessary for playing well with kids my own age. I was a dark child, fatalistic by nature and sometimes distressingly blunt, and I had come to expect emotional and social disaster at almost any turn.

"The prize really should have been mine," Louisa went on. "My poster would have won, except I took it home to work on it and it got ruined in the rain."

Sometimes life is just like that, but I didn't know that then. I believed her. Louisa was an artist: my most obvious skill in art class was eating paste. It made perfect sense to me that if I won something, someone would be along shortly to explain why I didn't deserve the prize. I thought about just handing over my winnings to her, *but I didn't want to.* I may have had the self-esteem of a rock, but I was in intimate touch with my own greed.

To my silence she said, "I worked on it really hard."

Her best friend said to me, "You should give her the money."

I kept it. I agonized over it from time to time: but I kept it. I felt badly that everyone in my class would hear that I was the heartless bully who cheated Louisa McFarland out of her rightful reward: but I kept it.

So what I learned from winning the poster contest was that I had no valuable skills as an artist. My skills leaned more toward plucking defeat from the jaws of victory, and barging through doors that were already open. I successfully avoided any opportunity to win by default in art contests for the next forty-odd years.

Still, I have always dreamed of being able to draw. People whose drawing skills I have envied aloud have said to me, "Anybody can draw — maybe you should just take a class." But my inner child cannot be so easily tricked. My inner child has always understood that the only art contest she ever entered she won because of rain damage. Ever vigilant against ego flares, my inner child can turn that advice right around to mean that anyone who does something well assumes everyone else can do it well because it comes so easily to them. In the years that I have shared my hopes and dreams with my Beloved, however, I may have mentioned my desire to draw a time or two too many because she began leaving around conspicuous little sticky notes with the whens and wheres of drawing classes. This fall I missed the registration deadline for all of the drawing classes, but I did sign up for and actually appear for a watercolor class put on by our local art museum.

I showed up for class with an empty bag. I could have brought along my two sets of colored pencils, the watercolor paint set I got for Christmas when I was seven, my artist's eraser, and my impressive paper and blank book collections because I own all of that. I love art supplies. I love art stores and always have. I am the only childless fifty-year-old lesbian on the block who owns three complete sets of the 64-color crayons (both the old colors and the new). My Beloved finally convinced me to take the class by saying, "Think of all of the new supplies you'll need to buy!" I didn't take my preexisting supplies to class with me, however, because for an additional fee . . . I could buy more.

I haven't drawn, painted, quilted, colored, or stained very much in my life because I am extremely vague on the concept of how colors interact. I have colored enough Easter eggs to know that blue and yellow make green. Beyond that, I am a photographer, not an artist—all of the colors I need in photography are already there. Our instructor murmured for a while about "swoozling" and drawing from the right side of the brain, and then she said to the class, "You need to be painting!" Someone handed me a child's miniature plastic muffin pan, and they gave me—and I am serious here—three shades of blue, two shades of red, and one yellow and they said, "Paint."

I thought about all of the things that are blue, red, or yellow.

Everyone else in the class began madly swoozling. Recklessly and completely without regard for the integrity of their paint they dipped their brushes in this color and then another, then into a glass of dirty water, and they made little piles of colors—pinks, oranges, magentas that they seemed to make up on the spot.

"What would you like to paint?" the instructor prompted me, and I sat there, staring at three blues, two reds, and a yellow in the bottom of a minature plastic muffin tin. I thought to myself, *What the hell am I doing here? I have no skills in art. I have to go home now.* It was only a matter of time before Louisa McFarland would show up and explain why she should have custody of all of my unused art supplies.

"You really thought you could walk into the class and just *know* everything they were going to teach?" my Beloved inquired when we discussed it later.

"But I didn't know *anything*," I wailed. "They kept saying things like 'blue is the coldest color'—what is so 'cold' about blue? I *like* blue."

"Have you ever taken an art class before?"

"Of course not," I dismissed. "I don't have any artistic skills."

"Maybe that's what art classes are for."

I scowled.

"I never realized life was this hard for you," she marveled.

We were teetering now on the edge of dangerous terrain. I was the kid who ate paste in art class in the fifth grade. I have worked, scrubbed, and polished my public self for nearly a lifetime since then, until, to the untrained eye, I might appear confident, relaxed, and even comfortable in social settings. I have a droll but amusing sense of humor. I have learned how to make friends. But buried deep inside is still a ten-year-old paste eater with one ear always cocked for those subtle remarks that imply I somehow overlooked another rule, that there's something about all that social interaction stuff that I still don't get.

"I can do this class," I said sullenly.

"It's a *class*," my Beloved said. "It's supposed to be *fun*." And I can hear my mother's voice echoing from the past: *You just never seem to have any* fun, *Sherry . . .*

I paid ninety bucks to take this watercolor class. First I'm going to order fifty dollars' worth of books about colors and all of the mischievous things they've been doing with each other while I wasn't looking. And then I'm going to go back to that class and I'm going to have FUN.

If it kills me.

scenes from a road trip

my friends and i are Midwestern women. The three of
them—my partner, Nancy (my Beloved), her sister
Mary, and their prodigal friend Susan—grew up in the
same small town: I grew up in a small town an hour away
and a couple of back streets wider, but it's all the same,
German/English/Scottish Protestant farmers with the
odd Italian Catholic thrown in for color. We are a practical people, not big risk-takers. (The big risk-takers, as
other authors have pointed out, migrated on west.) We
are suspicious of people who show off too much or
appear to be having too much fun. Dead Calvinists are
salted down around our roots. We are people who tend
our roots. We plant trees in our yard that take thirty to
fifty years to mature. We expect to still be there. We
expect nothing to have changed all that much between
now and then.

We are also women who, for one reason or another,
have had reason to look at that heritage not only for its
strengths but also for its weaknesses. There are relatives
not all that long buried in Nancy's family and mine who
would not embrace our relationship. There are relatives
still alive who would prefer we just not *talk* about it.
Susan left the Midwest years ago and moved to the

South, having always found the fit here in conformity-
land a touch too binding: she has come home for the
summer to heal after an emotional battering, but none of
us expect her to stay. She hates the cold—both literally
and figuratively—too much. Mary, whose life on the surface is the most conventional, has struggled with
Western medicine's curious indifference to anything that
cannot be cut out or drugged. She is still married to her
childhood sweetheart, a man she seems truly to love and
a man who has doubtless made her loyalty a challenge.
("But it's always been interesting," she will comment
later.)

We have driven a hundred and fifty miles to stay
overnight in a basement, drink bad coffee for breakfast,
and have our fortunes told.

Before I met my Beloved I had never heard of Camp
Chesterfield and, except for a brief dalliance with the
occult years ago, I had rarely consulted a psychic.
During that brief dalliance I took "psychic lessons" with
a group of friends, all of whom either possessed skills
and insights greater than I could imagine or they were all
crazier than loons, but I am not necessarily qualified to
make that determination. Many of my friends in this
class had spent their lives half in/half out of the psychic
world; I had once answered a phone before it rang. I
loved the idea of a psychic class, but my mind has never
been flexible enough to bend around corners. I *wanted* to
believe them. Ultimately I came to believe that agreeing
to spend time in a room where people are doing things I

have never done before does not automatically make me "open" to the possibilities. Sometimes it just makes me scowl.

My Beloved's friend Susan returned this summer — for the summer — after having wandered the far edges of the country, and while the two of them were exchanging stories and memories, they determined we should all make a trip to the tiny community of psychics known as Camp Chesterfield in Anderson, Indiana, to have our futures told. A variety of our friends were included in the planning phases of this trip, but when we left it was the four of us.

I am the youngest of the group, for whatever that's worth. I'm fifty-four. And I am an eldest child, a distinction that seems fairly benign to Mary and me, but which Nancy and Susan claim had not gone unnoticed. Susan has spent most of this summer with her sister/mother, who is seventeen years her senior, and she has already told me the caretaker/charge relationship she had hoped might mellow into sisterhood has remained as rigid and role-defined as it was when she was four. Susan has spots chafed raw by too much exposure to big sisters. Big sisters, Susan maintains, have no concept of what it means to be the baby.

Nor am I younger than any of them by very much. In order of seniority we are Mary and Susan, who are within months of each, then Nancy, then me. Age is not the issue and birth order hardly matters to women our age: like old hens in the yard, we just like to keep the pecking order straight. We are four women packed into Mary's SUV and headed for a psychic camp for a short weekend.

Nancy loves the SUV. It's big. It's white. It commands authority on the road. Drivers who might challenge her little green Toyota hesitate and give way to the SUV. It looks like a man's vehicle. There is no man in it or anywhere near it, but it muscles us down the road like a bodyguard. *Step aside, step aside.* We feel little and important and protected inside, although it is a proud member of the most dangerous class of vehicles on the road.

I had written an article about fat girls shopping for dress-up clothes that Nancy has me read to the group. She and I are women of size: Mary and Susan are not. Nancy has heard it at least three times by now (she also lived it) and she laughs at my best lines. She and I are in the front and I can't tell how the women in the back are reacting.

It's clear to me that appearances are important to Susan. She is a small blond, a configuration of color and appearance I have in the past jokingly referred to as "the enemy." Susan is not my enemy. My "enemy" is some small, arrogant blond who may or may not have existed back in junior high school or perhaps even further back than that. A stereotype gleaned from after-school soap operas or romance novels. My enemy is a lifetime of total strangers walking up to me to recommend diets their great aunt Sarah tried with amazing results, and she was "almost as big as you are" when she started. My distrust of Susan has nothing to do with Susan, the woman who is my partner's childhood friend, and it is not Susan's fault she reminds me of the daughter my mother wished she had or the popular high school cheerleading career I once so desperately wished I had. I have grown confident enough in my writing and angry enough about what presumptions about size and character do to all of us that I can read out loud about being as wide as I am tall to small and exquisitely proportioned women without gritting my teeth or flinching. I always know where they are.

We stop for dinner at a restaurant in downtown Auburn that turns out to be a cafeteria. They advertise "over 50 selections" on the way in. We settle in, order our drinks, drift along the salad bar adding bits of this and that to our composite. By the time I sit down at the table Susan is already talking to Mary, who answers, "I wore them for Bob because he was so curious about them."

Bob is a friend of ours, a gay man studying the ministry. It is a tribute to my affection for him and his tolerance for different points of view that he and I are even friends. (I have issues with conventional religion as well.) Bob was supposed to come with us on this trip but had to cancel at the last minute.

I study Mary thoughtfully, trying to imagine what she might have worn that my friend Bob would be curious about. I check her clothes, her earrings, I am about to duck discreetly under the table to check her shoes when I realize she has breasts. This gives me an interesting insight into my friend Bob, and I laugh. "You're wearing boobs," I note. "I like them—they look very nice."

Mary had a radical mastectomy four years before. When she was first diagnosed with breast cancer she studied all of the available information about breast cancer, implants, and their accompanying potential problems. She opted not to replace one problem with another. Now, however, she is considering a career change into an industry where conventional physical appearance is more important—she's decided to become a professional dealer for one of the local casinos, and flat-chested women don't get as many tips.

"I hate them," Mary says. They get in her way and make her feel claustrophobic. She is allergic to virtually all adhesives, and the breasts are glued in some fashion to her chest. "I can't wait to get where we're going and see what this adhesive has done."

Right now she works for a heating and cooling company where she is one of perhaps two women—the rest are all plumbers and metal fabricators, all men. She has never made any secret about her breast cancer or the mastectomy required to save her life. For all I know the men she has worked with know all about the $6,000 replacement breasts she bought—they've had all day to notice them.

The women in Nancy and Mary's family are heavy-breasted women, even while the rest of their bodies are, like Mary's, fairly standard. Her breasts have always embarrassed her and she has told us more than once she is perfectly happy flat-chested.

I don't know what to say to a woman who has faced down cancer—who is still facing down cancer—but I know that facts are more comfortable for her than emotions, so we talk about size. She tells about walking into a lingerie store and trying on bras, stuffing wads of toilet paper in them to try to decide what size she felt would suit her. She told us the salesclerks were all women our age who looked at her with silent panic in their eyes. They told her they had no idea how to fit her and called their manager, a pert little "twenty-year-old" whose friends were all alive and who therefore saw the whole adventure as a lark.

We are flying through the dark between Fort Wayne and Anderson. Nancy is still driving. She has me tell the group about my desk partner, a redheaded woman of size who was driving off some bottled-up hostility the night she was pulled over by a state trooper for talking on her cell phone while driving.

She saw his flasher in her rearview mirror, but she determined she had done nothing wrong and kept driving.

He pulled up beside her and waved at her with his index finger.

She ignored him.

He started "getting obnoxious," she told me, which I took to mean he pulled up beside her and edged her toward the side of the road, so she pulled off.

He walked up to her car. He said, through the two-inch crack she made for him, "You were driving down the road and talking on the cell phone at the same time — that's a very dangerous practice . . ."

"But," said my cubiclemate, "one that is completely legal in the state of Michigan."

"Still," said the trooper, "it's dangerous."

"Did I use the proper turn signals when I passed you?" she challenged.

"You did."

"Was I speeding when I passed you?"

"No."

"Then why did you stop me?"

"I stopped you to warn you . . ."

"You didn't have any reason to stop me," she said.

"Ma'am," he said, "get out of the car."

She said, "No."

He said, "Get out of the car."

She said, "You go call your supervisor and bring him down here—otherwise I'm not getting out."

He said, his voice very determined now, "Ma'am— get *out* of the car."

She said, "You don't have a leg to stand on and I'm not getting out of this car."

He stood there. He turned around, walked back to his car, got in, and drove away.

We all agreed we would have been peeing our pants in terror when he told her to get out of the car, and we elected her our honorary queen.

About half of the year, travel in Indiana involves the perpetual question, "Is that their time or ours?" Hoosiers claim the confusion is the fault of Michiganders who go on daylight savings time while Hoosiers stay the same. This is not entirely true, because "their time" depends on what part of Indiana you happen to be in: the northwestern counties match their time to nearby Chicago, which is daylight savings time in the next time zone.

We arrived at Camp Chesterfield at either 8:30 or

9:30, depending on whose time you use. Whatever time it was, the front desk for the dormitory was closed and so we were instructed to just go ahead and pick out our beds.

We stayed in the women's dorm. The women's dorm is a huge basement room filled with single beds arranged to make the best use of a big open space. Each single bed has a matching antique dresser. Each bed is made up with the clean linens from an estate sale. Everything is clean, everything has been used a hundred times before. Everything smells faintly of mildew. Almost all of the furniture in Camp Chesterfield reminds me of what my parents or their friends had in their lake cottages when I was in junior high. Lodging in the dorm costs us ten dollars apiece for the night.

Mary is sitting on the edge of her bed. She has a kind of *how stupid is this?* expression on her face. In each hand she is holding a purple satin bag, reminiscent of a Crown Royal bag, with a purple drawstring top.

"How's it going?" I check with her.

She holds up one bag. "This is what they go in," she says. Each bag holds a plastic breast. Each breast has a small transparent form-keeper it slides into.

"They're lovely," I compliment her.

"She's a container lover," Susan reminds Mary.

We come over to admire her breasts, which have not blistered her chest as she thought they had. Now she holds one in each hand. Each has a nipple and a textured areola. Each has a small flap that curves around her rib cage. The side that goes up against her skin is made of a particularly absorbent material that is designed to collect sweat. To wash them, she tells us, she has to let that material absorb as much water as it can, squeeze it out with a towel, and then lay it on the floor and gently but firmly step on it.

She tucks them into their shape-keeper and then their purple drawstring bags, tucks them into her suitcase, and then she just shrugs.

———

I would have to say, just as an observation, that psychics are not by nature businesspeople. Everyone who works and lives at Camp Chesterfield is a psychic. The desk clerk, the people who run the diner, the groundskeepers, and the clerks in the bookstore—all are psychics. Camp Chesterfield is a big grassy park, around which are a row of cottages two deep in a big U-shape, and in these cottages live the established professional fortune-telling psychics of the community. There are rules and regulations and politics involved in living in and owning these cottages, and in particular, what happens to these cottages when the original owners are no longer able or interested in living there. Since I've only set foot on the grounds twice and make no claims whatsoever to their world, they do not share their private workings of the community with me: I only know that there are the established professionals with their tablets out in front of their cottages where guests can sign up for a private reading, and the rest of the community fits itself in wherever it can, doing whatever has to be done while they wait for the acceptance and membership that has drawn them here.

But everyone here wants to practice their calling, not change linens or fry burgers.

We never checked in, and when Nancy and Mary went looking for someone to help them cash out Nancy started to say, "One of our group dropped out," and the woman said, "I know—your friend Rae couldn't make it."

Nancy just stood there, looking at her.

"You forget where I work," the clerk reminded her.

At 8:30 in the morning of an all-day moneymaking event the restaurant pop machine stopped making ice and was out of four out of the eight selections of pop. The breakfast line was closed at a quarter to ten because the cook ran out of meat, and the lunch line opened with a woman sitting at the cash register who had no idea how much anything cost or how to ring it up. It was all I could do to keep Nancy and Mary from vaulting over the counter and taking charge of the kitchen.

We were attending the first ever Spiritfest, a largely outdoor activity spread around the grounds of Camp Chesterfield where mosquitoes the size of bumblebees sapped the life force out of terrified guests. There were artisans selling their wares, musicians performing, and the grounds themselves, lush and unseasonably green, to roam—but those who ventured outside soon came back to the foodless, drinkless restaurant with giant welts all over their bodies and dark, sickly circles under their eyes. Rumor had it one driver lost his temper and thumped a mosquito and put a big dent in his bumper.

—

I run into a friend at the Spiritfest who gives me the name of a psychic I should consult. "He's wonderful," she assures me, "you'll love him."

The psychics who do not have cottages of their own have gathered in the far end of the dining hall, where each has a small table arranged with a clipboard for scheduling appointments, their business cards, and whatever small touch of grace they feel will give us a sense of their gift. One woman has thrown a lovely scarf with a dragonfly in batik over her table. Several other tables have floral arrangements. One psychic does readings based on flower petals, several others read tarot cards.

I sign up for the young man I will "love," and then I wander the grounds alone for a while to absorb the ambiance. Nancy has told me the entire property hums with the vibrant energies of the people who live there, and for a while I struggle to hear or taste or in any way sense this. I have never seen anyone's aura. I have never been blessed with any sense of who or what a person is beyond the obvious. My cat, from all appearances, has more insight into the characters who come to visit his house than I do.

It is more than wanting to know about the future or wishing I had more information about the present than I have. I want desperately to believe that the earth is one giant living organism bound by rules and interactions of nature both seen and unseen. I was trained to believe in nature as a machine, for every action there being an equal and opposite reaction, cold, bloodless, and utterly devoid of feeling: all of my life I have been drawn to those who believe in fairies or the earth as a sentient being, people who believe that animals, like us, have souls and feelings and significance that is inherent and undeniable. When I look into the eyes of my cat I see more than instincts and blood, I see a being, a thinking, intelligent personality that speaks and thinks in a language different from mine. I want and need to believe that life is about something more than the relentless production of crude oil.

What I find is Mary sitting on one of the many benches in the shade. She is people watching, perhaps. We talk briefly about Nancy, who is our common bond, and we talk about the flutes one of the artisans is selling and how Nancy wants one but will probably never spend the money for something so frivolous. I would spend money that frivolously, but I don't know enough about flutes or what draws Nancy to them to presume to make the selection for her, and Mary agrees. She would buy the flute: she does not know which flute would be appropriate, and she thinks the decision of which flute she wants may be that place where Nancy herself is undecided.

———

Susan consults a pet psychic to contact the spirit of her recently deceased horse, but balks when he starts giving her financial advice.

I consult the same psychic to have my dead cat tell me why my living cat is losing weight.

We go to the chapel and listen to a seventy-eight-year-old woman tell us about living with religion and spirituality. (My favorite part: "If you decide to take up meditation and you tell yourself, 'I'm going to meditate for half an hour every day,' I can guarantee you you won't be doing it by the end of the week. You need to set reasonable goals . . .")

We stayed for a lecture on how to contact our spirit guides. (We all agreed we liked the speaker. So far none of us have contacted our spirit guide.)

I consulted the same speaker to have him tell me my grandfathers both love me, I have a lovely crystal blue aura, and I am on the verge of doing something wonderful and amazing I haven't even thought of yet. I should open the door by taking a drawing class. I am to "embrace all sorts of opportunities" and keep myself open. I am a woman with a wonderful spirit — very balanced. I need to start looking to the East for inspiration.

Mary spoke to him as well. Ever practical, she summed up his message as, "Oh, you know . . ."

Nancy consulted a psychic who told her not to quit her job, to take kind care of her mother, and to stand up for herself more often.

Susan spoke to a psychic who told her to put her writing away and take out her brushes and start painting. She spoke briefly to the spirit of a lost relationship.

We sat in the pop-free, iceless restaurant and drank tea, compared our fortunes, remembered the lessons of the Midwest, and eventually talked ourselves out of all of it. The one bit of psychic advice we followed was directions to a Chinese restaurant.

———

Susan is temporarily broke. She came "home" for the summer to heal herself and to touch noses with her family and friends and historical home. I have never been anything but a coward, and I find the idea of being sixty, broke, and unemployed terrifying beyond all reason, and I suspect that fear—which is mine—colors my vision of Susan. Which is ironic: my own life is on the upswing. For the first time in a long time, more than the one same grim possibility shimmers on the horizon. Whether my career as a writer comes to fruition or dies on the vine, at this moment in my life I can entertain the fantasy of leaving my day job and writing full-time. I am inspired by hope, and galvanized by the knowledge that the worst that could happen is that I continue doing what I have been doing all along. The choices I would make would not do for Susan. There is nothing I can do for her but smile, make a fist, and murmur, "Go for it." And watch her go. My left foot will be planted firmly on the Big Sister instinct that continues to busily solve everyone's problems with the solutions that would work best for me.

On the way home at ten o'clock at night on the expressways around Fort Wayne we are pulled over by a patrolman for failure to yield right of way to an emergency vehicle. On three lanes of traffic he chose the middle lane to cruise to his next emergency and we failed to notice him and pull off into either of the other empty lanes.

"Didn't you see me?" the patrolman demands through the window. "I've been following you for over a mile. It's probably good luck for you that I've been called to a shooting because I don't have the time to write you a ticket."

We murmur apologies—all four of us—and thank him for his patience.

Once he's back in his patrol car Mary comments, "I don't think he wants to go to that shooting very bad."

Later I will learn that our newly elected queen, my cubiclemate, rethought her behavior and called the offending/offended officer's precinct and offered an apology. "His job is hard enough," she explained. Manners, which struck me when I was young as time-wasting exercises in the superfluous, have become the grease that helps us all slide through life more comfortably.

I never expected to be fifty. I'm not sure what I thought would happen. I think about my age from time to time much as children must stop and look at their bodies, noticing suddenly how quickly they have grown, how differently they move and follow thoughtless commands than they did the last time they gave it any thought. I keep looking for some logical explanation for my surprise. It's not as if I've been in a coma for the past twenty years . . . It's just that I'm the same person I've always been.

I expected something to change.

I remember when I was about ten or so I might spend a weekend with my grandmother and she and one or two of her friends would take me on one of their outings. They rarely went far—certainly never for overnight—but we would all jump in the car and drive away on some adventure. My grandmother and her friend Gertrude were avid indoor and outdoor gardeners and most of their field trips involved visiting nurseries or private gardeners who sold or swapped plants with friends. While I squirmed impatiently in the backseat they drove and talked about friends of theirs who had cancer, or whose husband had left or whose children were proving troublesome. Their conversations, even their destinations, all seemed so incredibly inconsequential to me. It was as if their lives had gone on and left them behind and they hadn't even noticed.

Now that I am my grandmother's age I catch myself wondering what *would* have seemed "interesting" to my childself. I shop for more plants for my garden every spring. I have friends—too many friends—who have stared eye-to-eye with cancer.

Now that I am my grandmother's age, I can see that there are advantages to aging that come on so gracefully we sometimes forget to stop and weigh their consequences. Aging people—aging women, in particular—vanish around the age of fifty. It's as if we begin to lose our very substance, as if the younger, allegedly more vibrant people around us can no longer see us as clearly as they see each other. We are like soap bubbles, fine and delicate and shimmering with rainbow colors around our shells until, SNAP, we're gone. Behavior that was once seen as a social crime, a misdeed that needed commentary and sanction, is now seen as harmless idiosyncrasy. We haven't gone anywhere, of course, but the young no longer see us as a threat and many of us have gotten over our need to actively police each other.

It is inordinately freeing to be beyond the critical scope of the young. I have no one I have to impress anymore. No one is even looking at me. What I once thought would be a terrifying transition—the loss of my sense of substance as a person—has turned out to be the time of my life.

when we were kids our parents bought something. I
have no idea what—a house, perhaps. Whatever it was,
it was *Extremely Important* and it *Affected Us All*, and the
three of us—the Wee One, the UnWee, and I myself, the
Least Wee—were stacked like stair steps on a bench in
some incredibly boring person's office and told not to
make any noise.

For hours.

Heath bars, brussels sprouts, and sharp cheese
change over time from stuff guaranteed to make you gag
to things that are actually pretty good by the time you
grow up—but nothing, absolutely *nothing* changes like
time. Elephants walked by, conceived children, carried
them full term, and deposited them on the rug in front of
us while we waited—not making any noise—for our parents to each sign their names twice. I was kicked eleven
times by the UnWee, who complained she was hair-
flicked twice and snot-blown seven times by the Wee
One. Our butts fell asleep, all feeling left our legs, and
the Wee One succumbed to whole-body bonemelt.
There was nothing left of her but a small gooey pile in a
yellow dress.

The Wee One always wore yellow, like the

UnWee always wore blue and I always wore pink. We were color-coded. We could have withered up and died sitting there without making any noise on that bench and our bereaved parents would have identified us by the few remaining strips of faded — but still color-coded — clothing fluttering in the breeze around our dust.

I remember this event quite vividly because I remember small explosions going off in my chest, not unlike Fourth of July fireworks, and banners started running behind my eyes:

CANNOT STAY QUIET ANYMORE
DANGER DANGER
CONTENTS ABOUT TO BURST

"Shut UP," I hissed to the UnWee, who promptly retaliated by jabbing her pointed little elbow into the pile of goo that once had been the Wee One.

The Wee One screamed as only youngest sisters can scream, an ear-piercing, nerve-shattering, end-of-life-as-we-know-it scream she reserved for kicks, punches, bites, and the occasional ground collisions accidentally incurred from older sisters.

Our mother came stalking out of the inner office (leaving our father to the endless paperwork of ownership), hauled the goo-pile off the bench and into her arms, and, thumping the traitor reassuringly on the back, glared at the UnWee and me. "I can't take you kids *anywhere*," she hissed, and stalked off to the car.

We followed, of course, because even though our

lives had been utterly ruined by the arrival of the Wee One, they were at least lives we knew.

We all crept silently into the car, each one hiding under our own window.

"I just don't understand why you can't watch your sisters for *ten minutes* without some kind of war breaking out," my mother snarled at me, establishing, of course, that it was all my fault.

In the backseat the Wee One was re-forming her bones and using them to idly kick the UnWee.

"When do you think we'll be able to go home?" I inquired politely of my mother.

"Please stop *whining*," my mother snapped. For years I walked around my mother as an attendant might a particularly unpredictable mental patient—one sensed that she was just not emotionally equipped to deal with three children under the age of six, although, I will add, it was not *my* fault that she had us.

Crushed by her constant criticism, I started to cry.

An expression crossed my mother's face—frustration, aggravation, embarrassment, perhaps even the desire to cry herself—and then she inhaled a deep breath through her nose, fixed her attention on something in the distance, and sat there in the car, idly tapping her fingers on the steering wheel while she stared off into space.

I wanted to hug her, or to apologize, or to snuggle up in her arms and let her gently finger my hair. I wanted us all to be a happy, loving family waiting in the car like movie children while our all-knowing dad bought our house. I wanted a clear, consistent set of directions for how mothers and daughters learn how to talk to each other and families learn how to experience life events as one organic whole. But someone had failed to issue my directions set and I had no idea what made families work together, so I slunk down underneath my window, tried to make as little noise as possible, and waited.

the vole hole

i work in an office building that has four windows to let in light for two hundred people. We are the Agency of Last Resort and our job is to supplement the welfare of society's most fragile members, so everything in my building is blue. The walls are blue, the cubicles are blue. When I first started the carpet was blue (it is now a sort of purpley/maroony/speckledy blue). Half of my coworkers are on Prozac. The building where I work has specially piped-in white noise so it always sounds vaguely like the wind is blowing. (This is to drown out the screams of dissatisfied children.) From the time I report to work in the morning to the time I leave in the evening, I have no idea whether it's snowing, the sun is shining, or the sky has turned green and is full of big, black, angry funnels bearing down on me. I can tell when it's raining because I can hear it on the roof. The roof is flat and has been known to gather several gallons of cold rainwater and dump them unceremoniously on poorly placed workers.

I do not work in this building solely with people. About two years ago a coworker was driving home from a long day of work when she reached into her bag to get something and a mouse jumped out, landed on the floorboards, and ran up her pant leg. She quickly identified this mouse as an unofficial inhabitant of our work site, and just after she missed the tree and the honking truck in the oncoming lane, she advised our Fearless Leadership of this incident. A few days passed without note. Finally the coworker decided to issue an office-wide mouse alert via our e-mail, describing her driving adventures and her unexpected copilot. She was awarded a reprimand for inappropriate use of e-mail. (The official charge was flagrant disregard of the chain of command.)

My Beloved works for a tiny private company out on the edge of town. She sits next to a window that opens. Beyond her window she maintains a bird feeder and all day long she is regaled with the music of happy, grateful birds.

A few years ago her printer stopped working. It just quit. It refused to go forwards, it refused to go backwards. It just sat there, making antisocial printer noises. Curious, my Beloved lifted the top of the printer to see what the problem might be. Every square millimeter inside her printer had been stuffed with oyster crackers. Some industrious mouse, determined to salvage as many oyster crackers as possible, had spent hours stuffing and jamming, poking and cramming oyster crackers into the printer case until nothing inside could move.

By comparison, the mice in my building are as eager to leave at the end of the day as we are.

In the back of my Beloved's work building, in the casement around the back door at the very bottom, is a small hole. This is a vole-sized hole. Actually, this hole is smaller than a vole, causing the vole who uses this hole to scramble and dig and scrunch and scrabble her way through for her daily visit. She comes to visit my Beloved—and my Beloved's daughter, the Girlchild—to beg food. (She's a vole on the dole.) My Beloved and the Girlchild have named this vole Velva. Velva the Vole. (Actually, that's not exactly what they named her, but it's only one vowel off, and even a vole is entitled to some degree of privacy.)

I am assuming that Velva was originally shy around people and made more discreet entrances at quieter times, but she has been richly rewarded for her behavior, and as a result, Velva has lost her fear of humans. Her scrambling, scrunching, scrabbling entrances through her own doorway are audible to the human ear. Frequently Velva positions herself near human feet where treasures like Cheetos and bits of bread might drop. If nothing drops, she has even been known to rest her front paws on the nearest shoe and gaze up, nearly blindly and vole-like, toward the source of manna. When she is given a Cheeto, her chewing is loud and not at all shy. Velva has come to enjoy lunch hour at my Beloved's workplace. She feels she is a warmly welcomed member of the workforce.

The Girlchild, concerned that Velva be given all of the benefits of an employee, posted a small sign over Velva's doorway that reads *Velva's House* so that Velva can receive her mail. I expect to find Velva listed on the pay-roll any day now.

I don't know what the lesson of this tale is, if in fact there is one. I suppose it would be foolish to compare management styles based solely on the way the staff reacts to small rodents.

a gathering of porcupines

the people in my family do not talk.

You can pick us out at social gatherings: we are the ones huddled behind the Wee One, poking at her with stray elbows and muttering, "*Talk* to them . . ." I am not sure when or why we appointed the Wee One our spokesperson, but we did and she is. This frees all of us to turn to those impaled on her rapier wit and say, "Oh, don't pay any attention to her—she gets it from our mom." My wit is no kinder and my Little Brother's wit is no less sharp—the UnWee's wit will slice raw meat—but none of us talk as much. Even our Baby Brother can curdle an ego in a few well-chosen sentences, but we have too many fond memories of beating him to a pulp to expect anyone to be afraid of him. We are like a family of mute porcupines, waddling about the gathering place, hurling quills at people who come too close. All but one of us are married to or otherwise entangled with partners who talk more than we do.

That one would be the Wee One.

The Wee One married Mr. Right.

Mr. Right is a monk. Well, he's not really a monk, he's just . . . very clean and serene. Once in my presence he muttered, "Oh, drat." And then apologized. (I can't remember the last time I settled for something as benign as "drat.")

About once every three or four years in the middle of a clan gathering he will suddenly say something, and we all stop and stare at him, and he shrugs and falls silent again. So far most of what he's said has had to do with the way houses are constructed.

He is our idol.

During gatherings when he is not around, we sit in small clumps and chant, "We want to be like Right."

For the first ten years my sister was married to him, Right and I had the same conversation every weekend.

"Hey, Right."

"Hey, Least Wee."

At the end of the weekend we had a whole new conversation.

"Bye, Right."

"Bye, Least Wee."

From time to time I might smile at my kid sister and say, "So what is it like, marrying your father?" I'm fairly sure that's more of an impression than I made on Right.

We have had Right among us for a while now. We've almost accepted him. Most of us can remember his name. Some of us—not all of us, but some of us—have accepted the possibility that he is never going to try to trap us into meaningful conversation, that we can just relax and be ourselves around him and nothing Bad will happen. This summer he and the Wee One celebrated their twenty-fifth wedding anniversary.

My Little Brother married for life. His first life was a little short. His second wife—for months I called her

Deb—has suffered somewhat under our reign of silen[.]
She feels that it's not that easy being married to a Peck.
She feels we are standoffish, a little, and perhaps not as
accepting as we might be. (We only know this because
she talks too much.) She has to be carefully watched—
there is just no way to tell when she is going to plop
down beside you in the middle of a family event and start
talking about feelings and emotions and interpersonal
relationships and the fact that her name, like the first
name of all of her siblings, starts with a P. ("P-a-m," she
pronounces as if speaking to the mentally impaired, "My
name is 'Pam.'") We have quilled her mercilessly, and
while she understands that she's been quilled . . . she
never seems to get it. She's been much easier to be
around, now that she's taking Prozac.

Myself, I was dedicatedly single for a long, long time.
I spoke warmly and with great enthusiasm about "alone
time," and my definition of a Perfect Weekend was one
when I never saw another living soul from Friday night to
Monday morning. I had my writing to sustain me. Of
course my Beloved, when I met her, had almost never *not*
been in a relationship. We are a match made in heaven.
She hates large gatherings of people because it is so much
work to make the rounds, talk to everyone, catch up on
what everyone has done and may yet do. I love large gatherings. I plop down next to the person I plan to spend my
time with and I wait patiently for them to notice that I'm
there. My Beloved enjoys small, intimate gatherings of
one or two very close friends—sometimes just the two of
us, locked in meaningful conversation. I knew meaningful
conversations were just traps by the time I was four.

iter, you say. I can see the scowl of con-
ce from here.

goal may be similar, talking and writing
y different paths to achieve it. If noth-
always includes the ability to edit or
erase before the final result is visible to the world. For a
child now grown who has never felt all that accepted in
her day-to-day life, writing has been a way to reach out
to those around her without risking the immediate cen-
sure of yet another social faux pas. Talking is a matter of
just throwing yourself out there as you come, naked and
unpolished, trusting your soul to the whims of the gods.
The world is full of people who are entirely comfortable
doing that. None of those people are related to me.

My family's amazing unwillingness to talk about
anything more personal than rain, the war in Fill-in-the-
Blank, or the rising cost of gasoline drove me crazy when
I was a kid. I had questions. I *ached*, body and soul, for a
meaningful and intimate conversation. With anyone.
About anything.

Tell me you love me.

*Sit down with me here and tell me all about sex so I can
think about something else for a while.*

Tell me why you married him/her.

Tell me how you really feel when he/she says that to you.

Is this what you wanted for your life?

A clever person would anticipate that none of these
potential conversational topics ever panned out quite the
way I had hoped. My mother, bless her heart, jumped on
her bike and pedaled away from the conversations that
could be had at her house as soon as she figured out how

to balance the bike, and my father was lucky to hear more than six or seven words spoken aloud in the course of a day. Probably what he did hear was womantalk and that held nothing of interest for him. And perhaps it is not fair to judge them, either. What you never learn you cannot teach.

There is that moment in every adult's life when a small child looks up at you, her small face trusting and full of love, and asks, "Aunt Cheryl, why are you so fat?" Suddenly in that bolt of sudden comprehension you understand where bad answers come from. I understand my parents much better now than I did when I was a kid. From a whole new perspective you think back (on virtually everything your grandfather ever said to you) and you realize it was nothing you said or did that made him that surly, he just hated you. He wasn't all that fond of kids to begin with and when he raised his own they turned around and came right back home with a whole new set in tow. Adults forget that something they say once on a bad day when they should have just given up whatever they were doing and taken a nap—and spoke to a small child instead—may be the one thing that child will remember, in full and gloriously unforgiving detail, forever.

My father was a total stranger to me until one day in my twenty-seventh year when I was riding in his truck over to my grandmother's—his mother's—for breakfast and he suddenly began talking to me. This entire human being just burst into full bloom right there in the cab while I was sitting on my own side thinking, *What the hell . . . ?* The possibility of the invasion of pod-people occurred to me more than once. *I'm sorry, alien, but you've obviously failed to do your research — my father NEVER talks about feelings, and here you are, blathering on . . .* My mother had just recently died and apparently he decided that morning that he had been stoic long enough.

I discovered that he is a fascinating man. He was nothing like any man or father I had ever known, but he was sensitive, he was in tune to what was going on around him, he was struggling to be fair and right and just in a situation in the form of another woman who had snuck up behind him when he wasn't looking. He was undeniably attracted to her, and he was undeniably a married (if widowed) man. And while I felt comfortable assuring him that my mother was no longer with us and would want him to go on with his life and be happy, I could see her stalking along the edge of heaven, scowling down at us both with disapproval just as easily as he could.

This suddenly eloquent stranger, similar in appearance to the man I had typically ridden ten, twelve miles at a time in the cab with in total silence, spoke to me at great length for about six months. Eventually he shifted his conversations from me to the object of his affection — where by then they were more appropriate — and I probably did not have another intimate conversation with him until seven or eight years later, after their divorce. Throughout our post-Mom period I have never been able to tell whether we are going to have a conversation of grunts or he is suddenly going to start discussing some twist in his life path.

When all is well with my father's world, an efficient

interviewer will quickly switch to yes/no questions. This is not because my father is particularly inarticulate: it is because his oldest daughter does not have the patience to wait ten minutes, fifteen minutes, two hours until he has composed his answer. (He inherited this from his father, who would carry on his snail conversations while the women in his family darted dialogues over and under him like rabbits playing in an empty field.)

The affirmative answer to a yes/no question is "Unh."

The negative answer to a yes/no question is "Nuh."

This can be confusing because sometimes "Nuh?" means "*What?*"which can sound quite a bit like "Hunh," which is a mischievous answer meaning, "*I'm not going to tell.*"

My father speaks very softly when he does speak and he hates having to repeat himself—in fact, often simply refuses to repeat himself—so true communication, while sometimes almost agonizingly slow, can turn on a momentary lapse of attention.

He is somewhat more difficult to communicate with on the telephone because he doesn't like to talk on the phone (see "repeating himself") and because that point when you lean forward, raise both eyebrows, and loudly clear your throat, indicating you expect some sort of reaction, over the phone simply sounds like you have a cold.

Just as proof that the Goddess truly does have a sense of humor, last fall my father had a stroke. He loses words, from time to time, but in particular he has diffi-culty remembering names. As a result of the stroke, he has moved to Alabama to live with his girlfriend, so if we want to talk to him, we have to call him on the phone.

I love my father. I want my father to know I love him. I want him to feel he can talk to me anytime, that nothing in my life could be so important that I could not find the time to talk to him.

But I am his child. Sometimes I would like to just sit back in a comfortable chair, put my feet up, and say to him, "Everything's fine. Take your time. We can talk whenever you're ready."

the stick incident and more

i was a miserably unhappy child. Some children endured a horrendous childhood to emerge as stronger and healthier adults for their experience: I survived the most uneventful Midwestern middle-class upbringing of anyone I know and emerged just pissed off at everybody. It is a skill that requires constant practice—not many children have the discipline to be as relentlessly miserable as I was.

Every now and then I will commiserate with friends about the horrible scars one acquires during their most vulnerable and formative years and my friend Rae, in particular, will smile at me and muse, "And how many times did your dad hit you, Cheryl?" She loves that story.

I was about ten, I believe. It was in the dead of summer when daylight extended on halfway through the night and we children would be sent to bed while perfectly good play hours lay wasting in the evening. My bedroom was directly over the family living room, connected umbilically by an open-air register that let up sounds from the television and, for the determined and easily contorted, sometimes even somewhat distorted images. First I was sent to bed hours before I was even sleepy, then I was sent back to bed from the register where I had lain on the floor and watched angled television, and then I was warned of dire consequences if I did not fall asleep immediately.

Exasperated by the shortsightedness of my parents downstairs, I fashioned my own amusement out of the bottom half of a miniature ginger jar and a red stick that had probably been the handle to something. I don't remember the point of the game anymore (beyond not sleeping), but it involved twirling the ginger jar on the top of the stick while rolling gracefully across my full-sized bed. Something went horribly wrong with the plan, however, and the ginger jar jumped off my stick and rattled incredibly loudly across the linoleum floor of my room, directly over my parents' heads.

I heard my father mutter bad words under his breath downstairs, and then I heard him lunge up the stairs and stalk into my room, where he grabbed the red stick out of my hand AND HIT ME IN THE BUTT WITH IT.

I was mortified.

My own father HIT ME WITH A STICK!

I disowned him on the spot, there was no doubt about it — I would hate him forever.

"How many times did he hit you, Cheryl?" Rae always asks here. A middle child of seven, a child of divorce with multiple remarriages of dubious merit on the sides of both parents, she finds the story of my abuse and misuse . . . funny.

"Once," I reply icily, because as far as I'm concerned, once is way more than enough.

"Once that time," Rae muses.

"In her LIFE," my Beloved corrects her, and off they launch into even greater gales of glee.

"He used to kick me, too," I say sullenly in my own defense.

"Like this?" Rae asks, and kicks at the air as if it were inhabited by a rabid dog.

"He would sort of . . . propel us along with the side of his foot," I mutter. "Ask any kid who was ever around him, they'll tell you."

"You had a rough childhood, Cheryl," Rae commiserates with me, but it's hard to believe her while she's laughing.

Beyond the Stick Incident, our parents rarely used physical violence to make their point. Our mother didn't need a stick—she had fingernails as thick as carp scales sanded into shape like talons. Anytime she sensed she did not have our full attention, she would grip us by the cheeks and bore holes through our souls with her yellow-green eyes. I was often tormented as a child by nightmares about this oddly maternal monster that howled at the moon and jammed raw meat down my throat whenever I cried.

My parents rarely drank, and when they did they became giggly and oddly childlike and then they went to bed. Often—with a great deal of shushing—they hid this behavior from us, although I could not always tell what exactly they had been doing because they fell into the same elaborate shushing behavior whenever they misbehaved. They were devout midnight fans of a woman comedian named Rusty Warren and often when we were supposed to be asleep they would gather with their friends in the kitchen or other places where they believed we could not hear them and listen to this woman tell jokes. It never bothered me in the least that they did this and it had nothing to do with my being dissatisfied with my childhood—I only tell you that because my mother would be mortified that I told you she liked blue humor.

My mother loved blue humor.

I told our mother the second dirty joke I ever heard in my life. We were not supposed to know dirty jokes, and we were particularly not supposed to understand them. We were to avoid bad words (which prevented me from telling the first dirty joke I ever heard). But our mother loved jokes and she loved to tell jokes, and what point was there in living with five little parrots if they did not fly home once in a while with usable humor? She laughed, and then she told me whatever people said before they started saying, "It's not appropriate," and she told me I shouldn't tell it a lot. I would lie awake at night huddled around the edge of my spy register and listen to her tell my joke to all of her friends.

I could not huddle *over* my spy register, where I could see better and hear perhaps more clearly, because sooner or later someone would murmur something about the comparative size of the ears on my mother's pitcher collection (as if her pitchers even *had* ears, big or little) and someone would yell at me to get back to bed. In bed I could hear the adults laughing and carrying on, but I could only rarely make out what they actually said—and I could see nothing.

I think I can safely say that whenever anything interesting, fun, or good was about to happen in our house, we were all promptly sent to bed.

When trying to force us to sleep through childhood didn't work, our mother reached for the teakettle. Someone had apparently told her that boiling her children would prevent colds. In particular I was prone to chest congestion and respiratory infections, and she steamed the wallpaper loose from the wall of my room. When more than one of us were sick she would build elaborate sheet tents around us and we would drift in and out of consciousness to the steady bubble of the teakettle on its hotplate beside our beds. Moss grew on our sheets. The Wee One grew tiny slits in her neck, just behind her jaws, and as a teenager she could swim two or three miles underwater before needing to come up for air. What she could not steam our mother baked with a drawing salve about the consistency of peanut butter, which she spread, hot, over our naked chests like cake frosting and then covered in gauze. (I've never been sure whether she was trying to keep our sheets clean, or maximize the degree of burn.) And what she could not steam or bake, she boiled in hot Epsom salt water until it healed or fell off.

While I am anything but stoic by nature, I learned not to flinch, limp, or otherwise show signs of physical injury or distress around my mother. She was apparently impervious to pain herself. I don't know how many times I watched her pour boiling water into a pan, ram her hand into it, and say, "See—it's NOT that hot," and grab whatever gaping open wound I might have accidentally let her see and ram that into the boiling water. A half a mile up the road the neighbors would shake their heads at my screams and say, "Oh, it must be that Eloise Peck boiling one of her kids again—you know, she still has five . . ."

Nor was she particularly understanding about my pain tolerance. I can remember sobbing hysterically at the very thought of blistering the hide off yet another innocent limb while my mother would roll her eyes up to the heavens and say, "Cheryl, I swear to God . . ."

Once out in the gravel pit behind our house, probably half a city block from civilization, I rammed a rusty nail into my bare foot. I felt it go in. I looked down at my foot, and there was a rusty two-inch nail hanging out of it. I hobbled on one foot and two toes over the natural bridge, around the bottom of High Horse Hill, past the snake pit, down the walkway between the North Pond and the Big Pond, all the way across the back yard and halfway up the back steps. A small herd of sympathetic angels ran along ahead of and behind me shouting for help and offering encouragement while I sniffled and upsucked my way home to my loving mother. "Mom," the herd of angels called, "Cheryl has a nail in her foot!"

I probably have not mentioned that there was some stupid rule about (a) going into the gravel pit (do not, I believe it may have been), or (b) going into the gravel pit barefoot (especially do not, it may have been). Like every child in the world, I assumed that if there were varying degrees of do-nots, then none of them could have been all that important.

My mother appeared out of the house where she had been either baking cookies for her loving children or perhaps reading one of the many novels she forbade us to touch. She picked up my foot.

I suffered in anticipation.

She aimed her talons for my nail.

I shrieked in sheer self-defense.

She slapped my leg and said, "Hold still."

She SLAPPED me, her own wounded child. I puffed up in righteous indignation, ready to point out that, had it not been for my noble courage and fortitude, hobbling as I had those many agonizing feet through the feral wilderness behind our yard, she herself might have been forced to venture out of the house to find me . . .

She handed me the nail. She laid it, like a small trophy, in my hand. "Why didn't you just pull it out?" she checked.

"What?"

"It barely broke the skin, Sherry—it's a wonder you didn't really hurt yourself, limping on that all the way back here . . ." She stood up and brushed off her hands as if they had recently been exposed to something unbelievably dirty, although all she had touched were my feet. "You'd better soak that," she resolved. "God knows what you've been walking through with that . . ."

I was probably my mother's most obedient child—certainly the only one who accepted, for its sheer substantive logic, the argument *because I said so*—so I never fully understood why injuries were so problematic for me. I had to hide the fact that I could barely use my left hand for two weeks not because I was afraid my mother would make me soak it but because I had accidentally impaled myself on a stolen pocketknife. I knew it was stolen because it had belonged to my grandfather shortly before it became mine and he had not been present when the transfer of ownership occurred. I felt badly about that, but he had a small collection of them and I knew in my heart that my life would have more value and be far more entertaining if I owned just one pocketknife. I had been walking through the gravel pit, admiring my new pocketknife, when a stone leaped up and tripped me and I fell down and jabbed my own knife into my free hand.

The fact that I wounded myself while under the spell of bad behavior would have so delighted her that none of us could have lived with her for months. Even worse, she would remember sooner or later that she had banned the ownership of small weapons in order to demilitarize our intersibling relationships and she would ask, "Where did you get it?"

I was not a stupid child.

I was not about to admit I stole something from her father.

My little sister had stolen a candy bar from a local store once and our mother had forced her to walk into the store, admit to her thievery, *give it back*, and apologize. (She is still bitter.) I would have died of gangrene before I copped to any of that.

Fortunately my grandfather did not keep his pocket-knives particularly sharp and it was a shallow cut that healed quickly. It did leave a scar, which my mother had also never seen.

Probably the most contentious issue between my mother and me was that of shoes. Shoes were the bane of my existence. In my prime I could walk across hot asphalt in August while the tar was bubbling and never feel a thing. I could walk barefoot on gravel, small stones, crushed glass, beds of rusty nails—I didn't care. Shoes, on the other hand, kept getting lost, or wet, or soaked in horse manure, all of which deeply offended my mother. I remember being sent out into the dark and nether regions of the back yard where the shadow-monsters lurked because I had lost my shoes and I would not be allowed home again until I found them. My mother lectured me about the cost of shoes, the value of shoes, the care and keeping of shoes, and provided me with a never-ending list of the horrible and maiming things that could happen to the feet of small children who failed to wear their shoes . . . As far as I was concerned the only good shoe was the shoe tucked safely under my bed where it couldn't get me into any trouble and I could find it quickly if I had to.

And so it came to pass, shortly after I impaled my left hand on a stolen pocketknife, that a pair of new shoes wore a blister on the top of my right little toe. This was somehow my fault—I had committed yet another shoe crime—and I was deeply reluctant to take this injury to my mother because *it hurt*. The idea of soaking it in hot salt upset my stomach. It was a fine blister, as far as blisters go, covering the entire top of my little toe and weeping some crusty yellow stuff with an unpleasant smell, but what bothered me the most was the pain. It pulsed. Throbbed. It felt as if an elephant were rocking back and forth on my toe, and I retired to the privacy of my bedroom where I could inspect this phenomenon in peace. The blister was angry and red and swollen, and there was a thin red line that appeared to be traveling up my foot.

I loved my mother. I never believed she intended to harm me, but I did harbor a slight trust issue. I spent much of my early life feeling like the cat in the elephant house and I spent a lot of my time places where she wasn't likely to be. And I was afraid of her temper, which for some odd reason seemed to go off whenever one of us got hurt, as if we just went out willy-nilly and wounded ourselves to make her life difficult. So I didn't tell her I had blood poisoning in my little toe because she would have been mad at me. I decided to cut her right out of the loop of my medical care and I pulled out my dull and not terribly sanitary stolen pocketknife and cut off the top of my toe. Whittled that blister right off. It didn't actually hurt any worse than the throbbing it had been doing anyway. And I never told her.

Most farm kids my age were steamed as children. My Beloved's family was rich—they owned a vaporizer. (The Goddess only knows how many siblings she should have had—the rest are gone without a trace.) When I finish telling my harrowing stories of being boiled alive in the interests of my health, most of my contemporaries join right in with stories of their own about mothers who numbed their hands washing dishes and doing laundry all day, versus children who still had feelings in their extremities. And when they have finished their own stories, they smile and look expectantly at me and they ask, "Why were you so miserable?"

I don't know why I was a miserable child. Perhaps for the same reason weeds thrive in the cracks in the sidewalk and wild orchids bloom in the damp crotches of trees—because it was my nature.

Whatever my misery was, it lifted, gradually, like morning fog dissipating in the sunlight. Perhaps I learned how to get along with other people and myself. Perhaps misery is ultimately self-limiting. Perhaps my brain did its own internal chemical adjustment.

My mother died when she was forty-nine. Since she left us I have never soaked anything attached to my body (or anyone else's body but my friend Bob's) in hot Epsom salt water. (Bob has a thing for bath salts.) I do not apply drawing salves to my chest, and I have difficulty enough breathing in greenhouses, much less under sheet tents of steaming kettle water. I have discovered that a well-honed fingernail is good for just about anything—spare screwdriver, thorn-remover, guilt-assigner . . . I never had any children so none of them will grow up to write about me. From time to time my nephew has talked to me about writing, but I always assure him it's more bother than it's worth. Nip that little tell-all in the bud.

I still don't like shoes.

self-confidence

I am fascinated by the arrogant,
not that it's a trait I admire —
I just try to imagine life without
self-doubt tugging at my skirt
like a dirty barefoot baby sister.
Dress it up all you want, she seems
to whisper, *You know it's just no good*.
I wonder sometimes what they *feel*,
the arrogant, while my stomach
churns and my faith fades and every
good thought I've ever memorized
vanishes in the blinding light.
How do they do that, believe in themselves? What stories did they read
as children, what astonishing success
did they achieve at a formative age?
Whatever could I have done so badly
that I have dragged the memory of it
clinging to my ankle through five decades
kicking at it every inch, every year,
and still managing to feed it better
than I feed myself?

shopping

i have never really been a trendsetter in the competitive world of fashion. I have a dress T-shirt and a casual
T-shirt. I went all of the way through college in a World
War II army field jacket (which, given all of the pockets,
was cheaper and more efficient than a backpack). In the
years before athletic shoes really came into their own, I
wore hiking boots everywhere I went. All through college I maintained just enough clothes to do the laundry
every two weeks and have something left to wear to the
SudsyClean. For years my entire wardrobe—including
my towels—fit neatly in a WWII canvas parachute bag.
I am fifty-four years old, and other than the occasional
panicked dash to womenswear just before a wedding, I
have managed to stay safely out of the cruel grasp of
fashion.

For about seven years I worked in factories where
whatever you wore was wrecked by the end of the first
day, so "cheap" and "durable" were the desired fashion
criteria. Even when I moved into the professional world
of office worker, there were still vague strains left of the
egalitarian sixties and seventies, and for a long time I dispensed food stamps and welfare while wearing jeans and

basketball shoes. High-tops, because I have weak ankles.

About ten years into my career as a nonprofessional "professional" person my employer determined I was in fact a professional after all and inflicted upon me a dress code. I can no longer wear jeans or athletic shoes to work. I can wear toeless shoes without stockings only between Memorial Day and Labor Day. I can be sent home without pay and ordered to change my clothes and come back if my pants are too short, if I appear to be wearing culottes or T-shirts with logos on them (although T-shirts without logos are equally illegal, it is a distinction that is repeatedly made), or if my toenails are unseasonably naked. I cannot recite the dress code in any greater detail than that—I believe it is a violation to wear bobby socks with skirts, I believe that has been an issue—I just dress as close to the bottom of the fashion chain as I can without getting busted and I've never risked humiliation and banishment over my God-given American right to wear denim in the workplace.

I wear stretch knit pants I acquire from Target for about twelve dollars a pair. I throw them out when the crotch falls out. I have several different colors but I could not fault someone for saying I wear the same pair of pants to work day after day after day. They fit. They're comfortable. They do not seem to set off alarms when the fashion police wander by.

About six years ago I happened upon a plus-size women's clothing store just as it was wheezing its last breath of business. It was a wall-to-wall sale. Clothes were 30 to 70 percent off. I spent almost $200 in that store, and walked away with a boatload of polyester work blouses that I have come to loathe. They wear like iron. Nothing seems to faze them. I left one wet in the washing machine for three days once—it bounced right back. About the only weapon that seems to do any destruction to them at all is fire, and while I can't justify ruining my own wardrobe, I have been known to cuddle right up against smokers, gaze softly into their eyes, and beg them to flick their Bic just one more time for me. The one thing these shirts seemed unable to do was to retain a button, but I was young and naive then and I introduced them to my ersatz mother-in-law. When these shirts are nothing but gossamer webbing fluttering in the breeze, those buttons will all still be attached.

Last year my Beloved wandered into my study and began collecting up the Great Unread. "Give me this," she said, and wrested unfinished novels, *Lavender Morning* articles, and scraps of poetry out of my hands. "I'm going to publish your book," she said, and—being my Beloved—she did.

It seemed fairly benign at the time.

Shortly after she published our book we sat there, looking at the boxes of unsold books we had published, and a publisher from New York called us and offered to take the book off our hands. She would publish it. She would tote it all over the country, she would sing its praises, she would *distribute* and *market* and other threatening verbs that sounded like . . . work . . . to me. I sold that book in a heartbeat.

That seemed even more benign.

Then my Beloved said to me, "Cheryl," she said, "you have to help sell this book. You have to go out there. You have to meet people. You have to autograph copies and have dinners with booksellers—you need clothes."

I am fifty-four years old and square. My bust, my waist, my hips, and my height are all within spitting distance of each other and as soon as I step into a three-sided mirrored dressing room they commence.

You'll never be happy while you look like that.

Honey, I just don't want you to grow up to be miserable and alone.

You know that boy you like in school will never look at you twice if you eat that piece of cake . . .

God, if you get any fatter I don't know WHERE we're going to buy you any clothes . . .

What an inspired formula: affection versus body size. And to think my mother could never figure out why I thought she hated me. All I had to do was look in a mirror . . . I can walk into a gym full of sprightly size twos exercising their brains out and ignore them like they're not even there: but when I walk into a three-mirrored dressing room in a women's clothing store my mother swoops down on me like a vampire who needs fresh blood.

And for all of the effort she devoted to keeping me from living the life of misery she herself had lived, I have done everything within my power to surpass her deepest fear. My mom dieted her entire life to stay just about middlin' pudgy. Me, I am FAT.

And I have learned to deal with that just about everywhere but in women's clothing stores.

Part of my Beloved's job is boxing up and shipping worms. She also ships books and educational videos, but it is the worm shipping that sets the tone of her professional wardrobe. She wears shorts nine months out of the year. She wears tank tops. I would kill to be able to wear the wardrobe to work that my Beloved wears, but they won't let you wear your own clothes in prison anymore and I look horrible in orange. It is part of the universal injustice of life that my Beloved has a very strong fashion sense that she is always inflicting on me. She, who could go to work in a burlap bag if she wanted to, is always picking on my favorite T-shirt because the "neck is stretched" or "what color was it when you bought it?"

My very favorite part of our relationship is when she turns to me and says, "Can I wear this to (wherever we're going)?" As if I would have a clue.

"Sure," I say bravely, and she smiles and affectionately tucks my bra strap out of sight.

So I went to a women's clothing store. I tried on several articles of clothing. I thanked the salesclerk profusely and I carried away a treasure. I took it right home and showed it to my Beloved. She blinked. She said, "What were you thinking of wearing that *with*?"

"I'll take it back," I vowed.

"Well, no," she said, "I just don't . . ."

"I hate shopping for clothes," I said. "The clerks hover over you like they think you're going to steal all of their eggs out of the dressing rooms."

"You need clothes," my Beloved said.

A week later I went back to the store. I told the store clerk I had recently published a book and now I needed the clothes to wear to sign autographs and have long, intellectual dinners with other authors.

She said, "We have a new line just designed by Bob

Mackie—you know him, he designs gowns for women like Cher . . ."

I flashed on some sequined number I had once seen Cher wear. Never mind that she was wearing thirty pounds of ostrich feathers on her head and the dress itself was slit open from her throat to her belly button; I tried to imagine eating dinner and chatting intellectually while various little rolls of belly fat peeked out curiously at my dinner companions . . .

The trip was doomed before it began.

"I can't shop alone," I wailed to my Beloved, "I don't *buy* anything. All I need is one simple little black dress and some stuff to perk it up—last night I went to the dress store, sped right on past, and spent forty dollars in a craft store on rubber stamps for my journal. I'm going broke and I still don't have anything to wear."

"Then," said my Beloved, "we will go together."

And together we went. We loaded up my Beloved's mother, my Beloved, our friend Rae, and me, and we drove to Battle Creek, where the same store that I had been to in Kalamazoo is purported to have better selections and a bigger sales floor. We were in a buying mood. We were loaded for polyester. The four of us strode purposefully into the store, the two clerks greeted us with pleasant smiles and said, "We're not locking you in, we're locking everyone else out."

It occurred to me to ask, "When do you close?"

The clerk said, "Six."

I glanced at my watch. It was 5:55.

"It's okay," I resigned. "I'll just go read to people naked."

My Beloved extended her longest finger toward the back of the store in an order even dogs understand. "To the dressing room," she ordered me.

She explained to the clerks that I had recently sold a book and I was going on a book tour and I needed clothes. She sent Rae scurrying to the trunk of the car where she just happens to keep stray copies of the book, which she dispensed to the salesclerks. She mentioned we had driven a long way to come expressly to their store. My Beloved not only ships worms for a living, she often sells them. A woman who can sell worms is a force to be reckoned with.

I went into the dressing room with one outfit. The next thing I knew four different women were knocking on my door, delivering outfits and extolling the virtues of their fabric, their design, and their price.

Put it on.

Take it off.

There's no sense wearing something that isn't comfortable.

Do you have slips/pantyhose/nightgowns/dress slacks/a top for that?

The two women who worked in the store, Brenda and Susie, opened a charge card for me, tracked down my old unused charge account, recommended designers, reminded me of sales, complimented one decision, vetoed another . . . We probably kept them an hour and a half beyond the time the store should have closed and they were unfailingly polite and good-spirited about it. I walked away with a simple black dress, a simple black tank top and a simple black matching skirt, five blouses and jackets to wear with them, two bras, five pairs of panty hose, two dresses, two slips, a work blouse, some jewelry, and a hat—very close to doubling my existing wardrobe—and a charge card bill for the biggest single purchase of clothing I have ever made in my life.

But I have clothes.

I have clothes I haven't even worn.

If only I had shoes . . .

the pagoda fund

i have been driving around all summer with about five dollars' worth of pop cans in the back of my pickup. In my old office, this method of recycling was considerably more efficient. I would wash my bottles, bag them up, throw them into the open end of the truck, drive them to work, park them in the employee lot, and by the time I was ready to go home they would be gone. Some enterprising thief would have acquired enough negotiable goods to buy cigarettes or a six-pack, I would have met my moral recycling obligations, and I didn't have to spend my valuable time sticking tin cans into giant can vacuums. I have come to see the spare cans in the back as a sort of cheap alarm system. If I go to the truck and the back is empty, I will know that thieves are lurking nearby.

I need this information because as he wobbles into his tenth year of service, my truck, Hoppy (or Hopalong, as I have affectionately named him), has become more and more eccentric. He needs a new muffler. His eyelashes only work periodically, making driving in rain something of a challenge. The driver's side door has a broken hinge and a sullen, frequently difficult lock. And I would diligently repair all of these minor annoyances if

I didn't also know that Hoppy—bless his heart—is on his third transmission at 147,000 miles and the symptoms of misfortune are becoming all too familiar. It would cost more to restore Hoppy to his former health than Hoppy is worth now. But he continues to run, and I have never been known to give up on a vehicle while there was still tread on the tires or gas in the tank. However, because the door won't lock (it will, actually—it's the unlocking part that's become problematic) Hoppy has become more vulnerable to thieves.

I expect Hoppy himself is fairly safe. When he was young and strong and got washed once in a while he was a beautiful truck, a silver-and-purple 1994 Chevy S10. He was the very first of his model and when we first went on the road together, total strangers used to honk at us and give us the thumbs-up. And he has held up well. He sags just a bit in the rear, but I'm probably the only one who notices. He has tiny imperfections in his coat. Someone lightly keyed the driver's side door. Someone else threw him into reverse just as a dead tree sprang into his path and dented his back bumper. Due to the bad exhaust system, he roars to a start like a true muscle machine. He might choke a time or two immedi-ately after that, and he does have that whining, something's-in-my-fan-belt sound that last time meant he needed a new timing chain, but he always *runs*. However, I have to be honest. If I were a thief, having just robbed a bank or an ATM, for example, and I needed immediate and reliable transportation, I would probably not steal Hoppy. I would probably pedal off on some poor kid's bike before I would steal Hoppy.

Still, I leave the pop cans in the back for the same reason people who don't own alarm systems still slap a "This Property Protected By . . ." sticker in their windows.

This morning I went racing out into the rain and jumped into Hoppy, noticing as I did that his driver's side door had not been shut properly and the seat was slightly damp. This was odd because I have lived with a bad hinge for a long time and I know how to close the door so the catch grips. Also, my souvenir button from a trip to D.C. to see the AIDS quilt was lying on the front seat, when normally I keep it in the crock on the floor. I threw it on the seat and roared on down the road.

I stopped at a drive-through to pick up my breakfast, reached down to the crock on the floor to get change . . . The crock was gone. The entire crock. Gone. It had not slid right, under my feet, it had not slid left, into the passenger side foot space. It was gone.

I thought, "What the . . . ?"

Someone had broken into my aging truck, parked in my own driveway, and stolen my pagoda fund. And they walked right past my pop can collection/alarm system to do it.

I bought the crock at a yard sale. Originally I was going to pot a plant in it, but to get it home I set it on the truck floor in front of my drink slots and a brilliant idea occurred to me—I would keep change in it. The crock was about eight inches across and about four inches deep, made out of crockery, and it was heavy enough to stay where I put it. (This assumption turned out to be untrue. When I step on the brakes too hard, the crock slides down and clips me in the ankle. So far it hasn't been a problem, but if I ever seriously tried to avoid a collision I would probably wind up in a walking cast. The possibility that the crock system of change containment may not be entirely healthy has occurred to me.)

I acquire change easily. I don't know why. I have probably $100 worth of pennies that have settled to the bottoms of my drawers and vehicle carpeting, and I routinely clean out my purse because it's filling up again with pennies. I could see that this crock had value. I would never be able to accumulate enough change to fill that crock (she said whimsically).

About the same time I bought the crock, I fell in love with a pagoda someone had in their garden. I had a pagodaless garden, myself. It seemed unfair. Some people call them Japanese lanterns, some people call them Japanese bird feeders, I call them pagodas. They are cement. They are a garden decoration. I wanted one. My Beloved said, "Save up your money and buy one."

My Beloved is always introducing foreign concepts into our relationship. I said, "What do you mean, 'save'?"

She said, "You put your credit card back in your wallet, and you set aside a small amount of money each week until you have enough money to buy your pagoda in cash."

I said, "But I have a credit card."

My Beloved smiled at me. "But you don't like paying the bill," she said. My Beloved can be mean.

So every day I went through the drive-through and bought my breakfast and I threw my change into the crock and called it my pagoda fund.

This morning some enterprising thief stole my pagoda fund, crock and all.

We already know several things about this thief:

1. He can't close a simple truck door.
2. He has some personal vendetta against the AIDS quilt. He stole my tire pressure gauge, he stole my open-ended wrench, he stole a string of Mardi Gras beads—all of these were also in the crock—but he threw back the AIDS quilt button.
3. He is desperate and probably dangerous. He's armed with a crock. The last time the crock slid off the rise and clipped me in the ankle I think it must have weighed a good ten pounds, so this individual—we will assume he is a man, a woman would have brought her own booty bag—is (a) not clever enough to realize the bulk of his booty was aged crockery (i.e., *heavy*), and (b) dedicated to the notion that he should get something for nothing. For instance, I have never toted the crock into the house and tallied up my pagoda fund because that crock is heavy. It was not heavy enough yet to have enough money to buy my pagoda.

On the top of the junk in the crock there was a see-through container that held my quarter collection. There was $7.25 in the container. There were other small containers in the crock that were not see-through. I suppose just looking at it from the top, that crock might have looked like a windfall. I'd like to be there when he shakes out my other quarter-shaped containers and finds himself the proud new owner of 3,000 gloriosa daisy seeds. And—as is true of all of my change collections—the bulk of the collection is not quarters, it's pennies, so I would guess all told this individual relieved me of just about $20.

I wonder how far he had to tote that crock to find that out.

I am not feeling as kindly toward this thief as I do toward those who recycled my pop cans for me. They were at least willing to contribute a little work toward their goal. Not to mention I've been saving for three years and now I'm $20 farther away from having my pagoda. And it's not what this thief stole that chafes—it's that he entered my space. He took my stuff. He defiled that tiny, safe part of the world that is *mine*—not to mention what he may have done to my Mardi Gras beads. The world is an uglier, dirtier place because of him, and I hope he sets that crock on his own floorboard, guns his engine, and makes a hard right turn.

nesting in dense foliage

according to my bird book, the house finch builds her nest in "dense foliage," which must be why there is now a little twig nest holding five little green eggs in my hanging begonia. There is a nondescript little grayish brown bird in the nest, and she has made it remarkably clear that I should stop using my side porch from now on. She has important work to do. It annoys her to have to fly away just because I keep using the door.

Last month I was not allowed to get my mail (different porch) for much the same reason.

Before I bought my new house, I had never seen a house finch.

In truth, a day or so after I moved in, I discovered a rare, second species of American goldfinch. (According to my Beloved, it was the female.) I spied several cedar waxwings before she identified them as female cardinals, and I was hot on the trail of a pine siskin when she said, "That's a house finch."

I had never heard of a house finch.

"Perhaps it's a crossbill," I said wistfully, consulting my book: but my Beloved began chatting irrelevantly about habitat and native vegetation and other boring stuff, and then she proposed the theory that exotic birds hardly ever come to city feeders. She said, "ergo . . . 'exotic.'" I suspect she does not have the imagination to be a really good birder.

I saw a Kirtland's warbler the other day, but she just rolled her eyes and walked away.

According to my book, a house finch is "a sparrow dipped in raspberry sauce." (This describes the male, of course: the female keeps a much lower profile. She looks like a wooden sparrow with all of the paint weathered off.)

(There are purple finches, as well. They look very much like a house finch, except they have white rumps. Birding, I'm finding, can be a rude sport. *Excuse me, please, but could I — ahem — see your . . .*)

According to my book, a dealer in exotic birds in Long Island avoided paying the exotic birds taxes in the 1940s by releasing his supply of house finches. Sixty years later, they are producing multiple families on both porches of my house in Michigan. Fairly adaptive for a bird that identifies a tuberous begonia as a native plant species.

I bought my new house in the winter.

I bought a bird feeder on a lark. It was a cute little wire cage that held something called a "seed cake." I hung up my seed cake, and it sat there untouched for three months: and then one day it disappeared. In the meantime, of course, I had read several books on bird luring, and all had warned me that my birds might take their own sweet time finding my feeder, so I was surprised and delighted when my seed cake disappeared over a period of three days. What wondrous birds must be living in my back yard!

And indeed, as birds go, it was nearly miraculous. It had four feet, and a thick, bushy tail, and when I mentioned I was suspicious it was not a bird at all, it scurried down the pole and sat in the snow and chattered furiously at me. So far, my Just Say No program for seed-addicted squirrels has been a screaming failure. I bought them two bags of corn, thinking that if I fed them something appropriate, they would leave the bird feeders alone. I tossed an ear of corn out in the back yard, and twenty minutes later it was gone. Corn, cob, and all. The squirrel, on the other hand, was hanging upside down on the bird feeder. (I found the corn several months later — he planted it, kernel by kernel, in my garden. I still find his work sprouting in the lawn.)

I was discouraged, I admit, but I reasoned I had not put out enough feeders. If one feeder is good, perhaps six is half a dozen. I bought a thistle seed feeder. I bought a sunflower seed feeder. I bought a mixed-seed feeder. I bought a ceramic feeder that fell to its death, fortunately, before the ceramic birds took over my yard. I bought a hummingbird feeder. I considered a flamingo feeder, but by now my Beloved had started to get ugly. She used words like "obsession" and "compulsive spending" and "instant gratification."

On Saturday mornings I found pleasure getting up, making myself a cup of coffee, sitting on my sunporch with Babycakes, and watching the goldfinches at the closest feeder. The cat and I were becoming one with nature.

It was about this time that nature decided to become two with me. I stepped out onto the front porch to get my mail and a bird flew away. It was clear the bird was displeased. It appeared, at least, that I could feed birds with impunity, but I was to stay off the porch when she was there.

Except she was always there. Every time I went to the front porch to get my mail, she made a big fuss about flying away. Finally I looked up, and there, in the corner of my porch roof (no visible foliage nearby, dense or otherwise), was a bird's nest.

I could only hope Visa would understand.

Now that I am on my second family (and second porch) I have spent some time wondering what Mr. Finch does for a living. He is almost always around. He sits in the maple tree by the sidewalk and sings long and fairly complex little songs to me if I happen to be in the yard. He—or his brother, or one of his 35,000 local cousins—spends at least part of his day on my sunflower seed feeder. I have never seen him on a nest, but then, I am not allowed to loiter in the area. In my Beloved's back yard I saw Mr. Finch procure seeds from her mother's feeder and take it to a teenager on the fence and feed him. Perhaps, like my own father, he deals with his children better when they are somewhat older. A week or so ago my sunflower feeder ran dry, and I took it in the house, intending to fill it and return it the next morning. In the morning I stepped out into the yard and I heard . . . I feel I can justly refer to these sounds as avian complaints . . . Mr. and Mrs. Finch flying from a bush to the hook where the feeder should have been, circling the hook twice, and then flying back to the bush. They were clearly displeased.

It was becoming clear to me that feeding birds is not as simple as "If You Feed Them, They Will Come."

I have entered into a contract, of sorts, the rules for which are quite strict.

The Rules

If you provide food once, you shall provide it forever.

A finch song is a gift of uncommon beauty, and all the repayment you should expect to receive.

Begonias are good. More, please.

Stay off the porch.

The fuzzy thing in the window should go.

one way to publish a book

in the beginning there was nothing but a series of pressboard notebooks shoved into a bookshelf over my desk. Every now and then the writing bug would bite me and I would fire off an essay or a poem or a memory, print it out on my fine word-processing computer, and add it to the appropriate notebook. I loved to write and I loved to accumulate things, so there was nothing quite like accumulating a body of work a writer could touch and feel and measure the thickness of with a ruler when the sense of accomplishment was hard to nourish. Most started as articles I wrote for the newsletter *Lavender Morning*, a tiny publication friends put out for the lesbian community in Kalamazoo, Michigan.

It so happened that my Beloved wandered one day into my computer room, examined my notebook collection, and said, "What are you going to do with your stories?" My Beloved is a woman driven to be all that she can be.

I may have given a shrug and murmured, "Oh, I should probably do something . . ."

"You know, if anything should happen to you, they'll be lost," said my Beloved. "You should publish them."

I could see it: I would die tragically one day, and the

next day my siblings would hire front-loaders to knock down the walls of my writing sanctuary and haul my sacred scribblings to the dump.

"I don't know how to publish," I admitted sadly.

And she said, "But I do." As luck would have it, my Beloved works for a small publishing company. The company—Flower Press—prints books on vermicomposting, the fine art of turning kitchen waste into fertilizer, but it is my Beloved who transforms eager young manuscripts into ambitious books. "Do it for your family," she said.

I held out my hand and she passed to me the red pen.

We spent one entire summer editing, spell-checking, compiling stacks of manuscripts edited by friends and relatives. We argued about commas (in particular) and the vagaries of punctuation (in general). We dispatched friends with piles of lumber to the table saw set up in the garage (we were also laying my Beloved's new kitchen floor that summer).

The world's most perfect sentence landed unceremoniously in the scrap bin beside badly cut kickboard. The sentence was beautiful. I could diagram it, I could argue for hours about what it said and the skill and language mastery with which it said it, while my Beloved held stubbornly to the notion that a "perfect sentence" would tell her something more than she knew from the sentence before. "I don't know what it says," she snapped, and four diagrams later it seemed clear to me I could maintain the sentence or the relationship, but not both. Still, I called total strangers and read it to them over the telephone, but it can be difficult to assess exactly how clear a sentence is by the way someone hangs up on you.

Finally we had the kinks ironed out, the errors in tense and number and style all corrected—we found the bonus sentence with the missing verb—and we were ready to publish. My Beloved disappeared for hours at a time until, finally, she emerged triumphantly and said, "Here it is!" And she handed me a CD.

"I'm published," I exalted obediently.

My Beloved looked annoyed. "Now we take it to a printer," she said, and off we went.

Weeks passed. I'm sure there were any number of adventures in printing that occurred during this time, but the printers called my Beloved, not me. She spoke to me from time to time in publisher-speak and I always tried to smile and look encouraging.

The (last possible) Friday evening before we were to leave for the Michigan Womyn's Music Festival we gathered excitedly in the front yard, each of us poised on the edge of our lawn chair, while the Girlchild raced to the printer. Rae pulled out her pocketknife in readiness while the Girlchild backed the truck into the yard and delivered unto us 250 copies of *Fat Girls and Lawn Chairs* by Cheryl Peck.

I was/we were a published author.

We sold copies of the book to all of our friends, all of our friends' friends, and six or seven passing strangers in the street. We hauled the book to the Festival and hawked copies to the feminist bookstores that had booths there. We gave copies of the book to our family in the fine hope that they would treasure and perhaps even preserve them. When we began to run low on inventory, we ordered 250 more copies.

Any number of very fine writers have struggled for years to have their books published by the conventional publishing houses, only to be turned down, sent away, and rejected. Many of these writers have believed so fervently in what they were doing that they paid the price to publish the books themselves, filled the trunks of their cars with books, and hauled them to every bookstore they could find. They convinced each bookstore owner individually to sell their book for them until their book began to build a reputation by word of mouth. Walt Whitman self-published. John Grisham self-published. To this day if you want a signed copy of a book by John Grisham, you have to go to one of the five stores that carried his book before anyone knew him, because he always makes a point to sign books for those booksellers. John Grisham may have been a legislator and an attorney, but he must also have had a lot of time to kill because bookstores are remarkably far apart and a starving writer could run out of gas between them. I did.

My Beloved took the book downtown to Lowry's Books, my favorite bookstore, and asked the town mayor and bookstore owner if he would be willing to sell our book. He agreed he would. I went down several days in a row to visit it purely for the pleasure of seeing something I had written with my name printed on the cover on display in an actual bookstore. Everyone in Lowry's knows me. I am probably known affectionately as That Nut Who Keeps Fondling That Book.

As sometimes happens in fairy tales and other unlikely adventures, at the time Tom Lowry agreed to carry my book he was in the process of opening a second bookstore in nearby Sturgis, Michigan. Many independent booksellers were struggling to keep one store viable, and *Publishers Weekly* heard about Tom and contacted him to find out what he was doing right. One of the things he told them was that he had a "little book by a local author" that was selling very well for him, and it was called *Fat Girls and Lawn Chairs*.

Five editors from New York publishing houses called me, leaving messages on my phone that they had heard about my book and wanted to see a copy for themselves. I took notes, copied down addresses, and brought them over for my Beloved to admire. She used them to ship copies of the book to them, a novel concept that had somehow escaped me in all of the excitement.

One editor from a reputable publishing house we had even heard of before wrote me a wonderful, warm, funny letter telling me how much she enjoyed my book and while it was not the kind of book her house was publishing, she wished me well in my career as a writer. We were so excited we had a celebratory dinner. My Beloved framed the rejection letter for me and we hung it in a place of honor on my computer room wall. We had been rejected by the best.

Editor Amy Einhorn from Warner Books called me and left a message saying she wanted to buy the book.

I decided when I was thirteen that I would be a writer. I do not remember it as a difficult decision: I was walking through the back porch of my parents' house and it occurred to me that I was thirteen and I had no idea what I was going to be when I grew up, and I thought to myself, "I'll be a writer." I bought an old typewriter from an office supply store for ten dollars, I bought a ream of paper (thinking, "I will never need this much paper"), and I started writing the Great American Novel. Hunkering down into my early fifties I had nurtured the dream that someday I would be a "real" writer, I would publish a book of great significance and import, and I would leave my day job for fame and fortune as a literary voice. I had, however, never actually *tested* this dream, nor, I discovered, was I all that open to the notion that someone else might test it.

I was terrified. I knew probably fifteen people who love to write, but none have ever published what they have written. All of the old self-doubts and insecurities began singing in my ears like the sirens shrieking at Ulysses . . . *Don't do it . . . don't risk it . . . don't take a chance now, for God's sake . . . What if you fail? What if it's a trick? What if they realize they've made a mistake, that they only* thought *you could write, what if you tell everyone you know you're going to publish a book and then the publisher backs out, what if/what if/what if????*

"What's wrong with you?" demanded my Beloved. "You have to call this editor back! I thought this was what you wanted—I thought this was your dream."

I curled up into a little round ball on her couch and started crying. "I can't," I wailed. "I wouldn't know what to say."

"You're a writer," my Beloved returned. "Make something up."

This is a highly guarded secret, so don't ever tell anyone, but the driving force behind my continued survival has not been my silver tongue but rather my ability to look pitiful and helpless in the presence of those who would serve my best interests. I applied this skill to my Beloved (for the very first time, I'm sure) and she called Amy Einhorn. In fact, the first five or six conversations I had with my new editor my Beloved had for me.

My Beloved and I had several worst-case scenario practice sessions, but I did eventually get to the point where I could talk to my editor myself, and *Fat Girls and Lawn Chairs* was released upon the unsuspecting public in January of 2004.

It's real.

I really did write and publish a book with my name on the cover.

I went on a book tour.

I've been invited to read my book and do signings in public libraries.

I still have my day job.

bonding

when i was eighteen and first looking for gainful employment, I cheerfully informed all of my prospective employers that I was looking for something "dealing with people." I was a "people person."

Where this peculiar notion came from remains a mystery. I had four friends in high school. I spent most of my childhood prowling around alone in the gravel pit behind my house. I am eminently self-entertaining and — as my friends occasionally point out — I don't have a great deal of patience with the capricious natures of others. I have friends who know, for instance, the name of every waitress in every restaurant where they eat. I don't bond with my waitresses. This is how much attention I pay to the people who wait on me: when I am sitting with friends in a restaurant and someone who feels they have not been properly serviced inquires, "Is that our waitress?" I freeze like Bambi on I-94. Why would I look at the waitress when I order food? I was looking at the menu.

Two or three years ago a little restaurant opened up within walking distance of where I work. The food is good. The desserts are to die for. The prices are comfortable. I eat there two or three times a week. I go there so often, as a matter of fact, that I learned the name of the waitress who worked there.

She immediately quit.

She was replaced by a woman who remembered that I always drink iced tea and who greeted me at the table with it each time I came in. I felt known. I felt powerful. Eventually I learned her name.

I never saw her again.

My friend Annie began joining me for lunch once a week. Normally we worked in the same building, met in the lobby, and picked restaurants at random, but then a long series of events began to unfold that put Annie to work for the summer in another building than mine. It just became easier for us to meet at the neighborhood restaurant.

Annie bonds with the carryout boy at the grocery store.

Annie bonds with the Amtrak passengers who fly past our windows each day.

Annie was impressed that the (again new) waitress brought me iced tea before I even ordered it, and wanted to know all about my friend, the waitress.

I knew beans about the woman. I did warn Annie, however, that it appeared to be bad luck to learn their names because they immediately quit. Annie listened to this, and then she began calling me "Eeyore." Annie bonded with the waitress, whose name is Sandy. They had quite a chat. I learned actual biographical data about this woman. I knew it would come to a bad end.

Sandy is an excellent waitress. She gives you just enough personal attention, she does her job, she keeps the floor hopping. She also told me the other waitperson was slow and inept, but I smiled because I too have worked around, over, and through the slow and inept.

Sandy also told me about her dental problems, and her niece, and her medical problems, and somewhere along the line, in my craven little Eeyore heart, it occurred to me that I knew too much about my waitress. I was expected to actually *remember* her condition from one meal to the next.

I mentioned this to Annie.

She told me I had a dark soul.

She scolded me.

She said, "You're just being strange."

The slow, inept waitress quit, and Sandy arranged to have her friend Luanne come to work there. Luanne was a good waitress, Sandy assured us—they had worked together for ten years in another restaurant.

The restaurant is not much bigger than a postage stamp. It may have fifteen two-person tables. Waitresses stake out certain tables as "theirs," and this is how, I presume, they keep from tearing each other's hair out in the kitchen. Two times in a row I sat down in Luanne's section. The second time Sandy walked by and said, "I don't think you like me anymore."

I whined to Annie, "I just want to go there to EAT— I don't want to do psychiatric counseling for my waitress before I get my lunch."

Annie called me a blackguard and told me to "just shut up."

So for three weeks I would walk into the restaurant and freeze in the doorway and wait until Sandy gave me a sign as to which tables were "hers" that day (because they alternate every other day and you'd need a chart not unlike those football coaches carry around just to know where the hell to sit down . . .)

Last Wednesday Annie and I went to lunch at the restaurant. We froze obediently in the doorway. Sandy gave us the sign. We sat down at the appropriate table. We ordered, got our soups, and with our sandwiches Sandy said, "Luanne just asked me if you guys don't like her anymore because you always sit at my table."

I looked up silently at Annie.

Annie said, "Hush."

Sandy said, "I just told her it was an accident, because I don't like to hurt anyone's feelings." She looked at me. She seemed to be waiting for something.

I ate my sandwich. I may have actually torn pieces off with my bare teeth. I thought of any number of quick, witty things I could have said, but none of them would have gotten me better service from Sandy. I'd be lucky if I could get her to pour hot coffee in my lap.

Annie babbled something sympathetic, and Sandy went about her merry way.

I looked at Annie.

Annie said, "Just don't say anything."

I gazed solemnly at Annie.

She said, "Okay, so you're right. Now—just don't say anything . . ."

Within the realm of human interactions, the fact that my waitress wants a friend and I want a grilled cheese sandwich is not of overwhelming import. The fact that I can be as quirky as the rest of my friends may have come as a horrid shock to me, but none of them seem surprised. And I doubt if Sandy realizes that she has effectively told me that every time I walk into her restaurant I now have to consciously choose whether to hurt her feelings or Luanne's (or what the simplest, *simplest* solution to that problem would be).

I keep thinking this whole situation should have just never come up—all I ever wanted from ANY of these people was my lunch.

I feel I'm paying too much for it.

gramma lucille

it is not reassuring for small children to watch their grandmother stab huge animals in the ass with a pitchfork, it just sets a bad tone. My Grandmother Peck raised dairy cows. Big, sullen, occasionally bellicose animals she prodded here and there with the tines of her pitchfork. Occasionally she had them killed, and then we had to go down to the meat locker and drag them home again in hundreds of little white paper packages tied with string. *This is Bessie—you remember Bessie, don't you?* Farm people just deal with that kind of stuff. I was not a farm kid. My mother bought my hamburgers from the local grocery store and she never made me remember their names.

Oddly enough, I have only vague memories of my father's mother when I was a child. Not all of them are pleasant. She tended to be a little sharp with kids. With me, anyway. She made excellent oatmeal-raisin cookies, which she froze for emergencies such as visits from grandchildren. Frankly, it would have suited me better if she had thawed them before she gave them to me. She was a large woman, particularly when I lived closer to the floor, and being younger, she moved faster and less predictably than my other grandmother. I always felt a little like the cat around her.

My grandfather suffered a heart attack when I was still quite young and his life after that was one of slow, steady decline. Eventually they gave up farming and sold off the cows because he could no longer help and my grandmother could not run the farm and look after him at the same time. She told me that when I was very young, my grandfather used to play cards with me and we had splendid times together, that at least for a while I was the apple of his eye. I have no memory of that. I remember a man who almost never talked, and who, when he did talk, talked slowly, often incorporating agonizingly long periods of silence and reflection into his conversation that were almost impossible for a six- or eight-year-old to sit through. By the time I was ten I would have milked cows with my bare hands to get out of having to talk to my grandfather. And I was terrified of cows.

He died when I was fifteen. I remember his funeral because I kept waiting for some overpowering sense of grief to take hold of me (I was fifteen: emotions were pointless unless they were overpowering), yet none did. I remember his funeral because my father, the cornerstone of stoic Gary Cooper/John Wayne-ish Manhood upon which our family unit was built, burst into tears and was so overcome with grief that had my mother not been there to catch him, he would have fallen on the ground. I had never seen my father cry. I had never seen a tear roll down his cheek before, and there he was, disintegrating before my very eyes.

I was neither a particularly astute nor sensitive child at fifteen: in fact, almost everything that I remember happening when I was fifteen was about me. I suppose there were other people in the world—there are enough of them now—but like twelve, thirteen, fourteen, sixteen, and seventeen, it was a difficult year and I had my hands full of my own concerns. I must have found some way to quiz my mother about my father's behavior at the funeral (my father and I found just living in the same house challenging enough, forget complex emotional interactions). She said that my father and his father had never talked to each other while they were both alive, and now they never would. I found that very poignant. I probably wandered off into the gravel pit and wrote a story in my head about it. I was not foolhardy enough to try to talk to my own father.

I went on about my life. I noted that my grandmother, who had suffered from a bad heart when I was a child and who frequently spent most of each winter in bed on the living room couch, appeared to recover shortly after my grandfather died of his. (She always suffered from depression in the winter: she learned to cope with it more effectively when it was identified as seasonal affective disorder.) I went on to college, got my degree, and eventually came home.

My adventures in college had not all been a roaring success. In high school I had teetered on the edge of the black pit of depression, but initially the excitement of going away to school, of confronting new and challenging ideas, pulled me away. I suspected my hometown of being excessively conservative and conformist and I was anxious to embrace the diverse and eclectic world of the university: it did not occur to me that I could put my fundamental definition of "normal" at risk. I began to lose my internal sense of balance. Three-quarters of the way through my college career, I fell into a black hole. There were days in my last year of school when I could not bring myself to leave my dorm room. When I should have been planning my bright new career as a college graduate, I was struggling to survive the day. I graduated and I came home again shaken and scared and depressed, with no idea what to do with my life. Something was wrong but I did not have the tools or the skills to identify or deal with it. And I was too tired. I got an apartment, got a cat, got a job in a local factory. For a long time I worked nights.

About the only person who was around, awake, and able to socialize when I got off work in the morning was my grandmother. I would go over to her house and we would have breakfast together and talk about houseplants, gardening, ceramics, and my desire to write the Great American Novel. She told me she also had written a book once, but I never saw it. I tried: I could never get her to show it to me. We went on gradually to talk of other things. My mother. Her mother. As I struggled with the thoughtseed that I too easily enjoyed women and had to work too hard to like men, my grandmother chatted on happily about her own theory that many women probably should have been lesbians. She had any number of women friends who would have been much better off if they had walked away from their marriages and pursued their affections for their friends. It was fine with her. It was also a secret she kept like a thousand other secrets because—while she would entertain any manner of idea while talking to a stray and possibly lost grandchild—she had very strict and unforgiving standards for her job as the grande dame of the family.

Long accustomed to storing "good" feelings here and "bad" feelings there, I found no real conflict with the notion that she led a double life. I can remember telling my sisters, "You don't really know her—you have to sit down and talk to her when no one else is around because she's a completely different person then," but neither of my sisters appreciate complexity for complexity's sake. She had offended the UnWee in ways that will not be resolved in this lifetime, and the Wee One and my grandmother together in one room put some very strong, outspoken opinions at odds with each other too often for comfort.

I loved her. She was there for me during a time in my life when I did not have a great deal left to extend to a hostile audience and I had a pathetic shortage of friends. She taught me to understand and cherish the bonds that older and younger women can share when they are willing.

She also played me.

It is a virtue that has fallen out of favor within my lifetime: at one time women prided themselves on their ability to manipulate the people around them. They "ruled from behind," and their skills at getting the men in their lives—anyone in their lives—to do the things they wanted done without their having to ask . . . these skills had value. They were skills to be practiced, like a geisha practices the sweeps of her fan.

I was leaving my grandmother's house one day and she followed me out onto the back porch and said wistfully, "I wish your father would do something about these steps."

I had not yet met the man. He had always been around, but he only liked children under the age of two and over the age of twenty-two and I had been his flesh and blood, too old to cherish and too young to talk to for far too long. I remember thinking, *Well darn that man.* "What is it you want him to do?" I asked, resolved that I could negotiate a peaceful settlement.

She wanted a railing on the steps. She had lost her balance and almost fallen, and with her bad knee the steps had become a treacherous obstacle for her.

I hunted up my father and I said, "Why won't you put a railing on Gramma's back steps for her?"

He looked at me as if I had slapped him in the face, and he said—as he always says when he's confused—"What?"

I capitulated. "Gramma needs a railing on her back steps," I said, "she needs something to hang on to because her knee isn't very stable anymore."

And my father scowled and he said, "I wish she would just *ask* me," and he stalked off. To find tubing to build his railing out of, as it turned out, because all she had to do was express the slightest desire for something and it was custom built for her by the end of the day . . .

"You never asked him," I accused her. "You used me to get him to do something and you made me look like an idiot because you never asked him to do it in the first place."

"He does so much for me," she suffered. "I hate to be a bother to him."

"Oh, bullshit," I dismissed—because I knew by then that she found some odd vicarious pleasure in my bad language. "You'd be less of a 'bother' to him if you just asked him for what you want instead of using me or anybody who walks past your web to ask him for you."

She studied me for a long silence, measuring her options. Eventually she smiled. "But," she said, pleased with herself, "you did it."

When I was a kid she always tried to get me to call her "Gramma Lucille." I never did, because for some reason I could never remember "Lucille" (I couldn't remember the right word for "pickle" at the same age, and every time I asked for one someone would give me an olive). She told me that when she died she wasn't going to go to heaven, she was going to go sit on her headstone and watch the rest of us. I would hope that heaven offers more challenging options than that, but whenever I drive past her headstone, I always wave and murmur, "Gramma Lucille."

fatso

my friend annie and i were having lunch and we fell into a discussion of people of size. She told me she had gone to the fair with a friend of hers who is a young man of substance, and while he was standing in the midway, thinking about his elephant ear, someone walked past him, said, "You don't need to eat that," and kept on walking away. Gone before he could register what had been said, much less formulate a stunning retort.

And that person was probably right: he did not need to eat that elephant ear. Given what they are made of, the question then becomes: Who *does* need to eat an elephant ear? And to what benefit? Are elephant ears inherently better for thin people than for fat ones? Do we suppose that that one particular elephant ear will somehow alter the course of this man's life in some way that all of the elephant ears before it, or all of the elephant ears to follow, might not? And last but not least, what qualifies any of us for the mission of telling other people what they should or should not eat?

I have probably spent most of my life listening to other people tell me that as a middle-class white person, I have no idea what it is like to be discriminated against. I have never experienced the look that tells me I am not welcome, I have never been treated rudely on a bus, I have never been reminded to keep my place, I have never been laughed at, ridiculed, threatened, snubbed, not waited on, or received well-meaning service I would just as soon have done without. I have never had to choose which streets I will walk down and which streets I will avoid. I have never been told that my needs cannot be met in this store. I have never experienced that lack of social status that can debilitate the soul.

My feelings were not hurt when I was twelve years old and the shoe salesman measured my feet and said he had no women's shoes large enough for me, but perhaps I could wear the boxes.

I have never been called crude names, like "fatso" or "lardbucket" or "fatass." My nickname on the school bus was never "Bismarck," as in the famous battleship. No one ever assumed I was totally inept in all sports except those that involved hitting things because—and everyone knows—the more weight you can put behind it, the farther you can kick or bat or just bully the ball.

I have never picked up a magazine with the photograph of a naked woman of substance on the cover, to read, in the following issue, thirty letters to the editor addressing sizism, including the one that said, "She should be ashamed of herself. She should go on a diet immediately and demonstrate some self-control. She is going to develop diabetes, arthritis, hypertension, and stroke, she will die an ugly death at an early age and she will take down the entire American health system with her." And that would, of course, be the only letter I remember. I would not need some other calm voice to say, "You don't know that—and you don't know that the same fate would not befall a thin woman."

No one has ever assumed I am lazy, undisciplined, prone to self-pity, and emotionally unstable purely based on my size. No one has ever told me all I need is a little self-discipline and I too could be thin, pretty—a knockout, probably, because I have a "pretty face"—probably very popular because I have a "good personality." My mother never told me boys would never pay any attention to me because I'm fat.

I have never assumed an admirer would never pay any attention to me because I'm fat. I have never mishandled a sexual situation because I have been trained to think of myself as asexual. Unattractive. Repugnant.

Total strangers have never walked up to me in the street and started to tell me about weight loss programs their second cousin in Tulsa tried with incredible results, nor would they ever do so with the manner and demeanor of someone doing me a nearly unparalleled favor. I have never walked across a parking lot to have a herd of young men break into song about loving women with big butts. When I walk down the street or ride my bicycle, no one has ever hung out the car window to yell crude insults. When I walk into the houses of friends I have never been directed to the "safe" chairs as if I just woke up this morning this size and am incapable of gauging for myself what will or will not hold me.

I have never internalized any of this nonexistent presumption of who I am or what I feel. I would never discriminate against another woman of substance. I would never look at a heavy person and think, "self-pitying, undisciplined tub of lard." I would never admit that while I admire beautiful bodies, I rarely give the inhabitants the same attention and respect I would a soul mate because I do not expect they would ever become a soul mate. I would never tell you that I was probably thirty years old before I realized you really *can* be too small or too thin, or that the condition causes real emotional pain.

I have never skipped a high school reunion until I "lose a few pounds." I have never hesitated to reconnect with an old friend. I will appear anywhere in a bathing suit. If my pants split, I assume—and I assume everyone assumes—it was caused by poor materials.

I have always understood why attractive women are offended when men whistle at them.

I have never felt self-conscious standing next to my male friend who is five foot ten and weighs 145 pounds.

I am not angry about any of this.

the enchantment factor

for my birthday my Beloved gave me a Dremel.

I have wanted a Dremel for a long time. And indeed, as I have shared the news of my Beloved's gift, my friends have responded "(slight sigh) I've always *wanted* one of those," or "What's a Dremel?" I have no idea what a Dremel is. It's a power tool. According to the box, it's a "rotary tool." It is not necessary to know what a Dremel is to want one. It is small. It is neat. It runs on electricity (although there is a rechargeable Dremel with its own battery pack). It comes with a lively assortment of bits and brushes and little felt things that look important and practical. A Dremel is an *instrument*: it is the sort of handy, pragmatic little tool that one eyes and murmurs reverently, "That would be *good* for something."

My father has a Dremel. My father has two separate buildings filled with tools. I suspect that—had he so desired—he could have lived a full and complete life Dremel-free, his routers and drills and buffers filling in those spaces that the missing Dremel left, but I believe— and there is a note of bitterness here—that he has not one Dremel but two. I first fell in love with the whole idea of a Dremel when I found one nesting in a small plastic box, its bits and brushes lined up cozily next to it, in one of his two tool buildings. ("Shed" does not properly describe my father's tool storage units. One of his "sheds" is the leftover part of a house.) I said, "What does this do, Dad?" The answer, as I recall, was vague. Several years later we were clearing out his mother's house after she went into a nursing home and I found her Dremel, which, he maintained, he had purchased for her and therefore now owned by default. He already had one, but it seemed inappropriate to covet my grandmother's rotary tool while we were unraveling her life.

My grandmother requested a Dremel to use to build furniture for her dollhouse. Since her dollhouse was furnished, I can only assume she did use it.

I have never seen my father use either one of his Dremels. Once, perhaps. He may have used it to cut out the inner lining of a plastic case I bought for a quarter. The inner plastic lining was molded to hold something, but the something had been sold long before I came along, and I did not have, nor could I even identify, the something that was no longer there. I wanted to use the case for something else. So he Dremeled out the inside. It looked like work to me.

My Beloved has a Dremel, although it appears to have run off to live with one of her friends and has been reluctant to return home. My Beloved used her Dremel once, to her recollection: she drilled a hole in her big toenail with it. Intentionally. This is not high on my list of potential Dremel uses.

A day or so after I received my Dremel I reported to my dentist to have my teeth cleaned, and as the dental assistant fired up her handheld tool I thought to myself,

"I could do this at home—all I really need is a packet of that peppermint-flavored sand she uses . . ."

I will probably do that right after I drill a hole in my big toenail.

Dremels are exceptionally handy for sawing off the ends of bolts that stick out and get in the way. Should I ever be pestered by an obstreperous bolt end, I am now prepared.

The Dremel company appears not to be wholly ignorant of the enchantment factor that endears their rotary tool to potential buyers. Packed inside the Dremel box are three pieces of literature: a small Dremel manual, explaining carefully in three languages that Dremels should not be used in the bathtub or to sever their own cords, and carefully—almost painfully—clarifying the differences between a Dremel and an electric drill; a smaller book of all of the delightful accessories and attachments the proud new owner can now purchase for their Dremel; and a third book—by far the thickest of the three—entitled "175+ Uses for a Rotary Tool." This presumes that the average Dremel owner purchased their rotary tool in an anticipation of some as yet unidentified need, and it is the responsibility of the manufacturer to clarify what that need might be, thus tidily eliminating the possibility of buyer's remorse.

At the Web site www.dremel.com there is an ongoing contest for new and creative uses for one's Dremel. I have frankly not explored this particular page of the Web site: myself, I have been scrolling around, trying to locate that beige plastic case with the internal plastic moldings designed to nest my Dremel. It appears that one can buy a Dremel in a case, or one can buy an uncased Dremel, but one cannot buy an unDremeled case. This flies in the face of intelligent marketing. Since I estimate that a full 50 percent of all Dremels sold never leave their cases, it seems foolish that the case is the one accessory a Dremel owner cannot buy. It's a question of need.

tin-foiled again

upon reflection it has occurred to Babycakes that he could have chosen a better person to feed, shelter, be-litter, and amuse him. He will stay with Mommy, he has decided (if with a slight sigh) — for in truth, he has seconds of genuine fondness for her (particularly those seconds around 3 a.m.) — but it is only because he is a fine young cat that he has learned to forgive her for her faults.

For instance, she deliberately deprives him of his favorite food group, chocolate. Mommy puts warm chocolate in a cup and drinks it, and she will not share with her beloved Babycakes. Mommy eats soft chocolate out of tiny plastic dishes that are just deeper than his tongue is long and she will only give him these dishes when the chocolate is more than tongue-deep. She is a bad Mommy, but Babycakes is a cat of uncommon inner personal strength, and he has learned to forage on his own.

Mommy has a round thing where she hides everything that might be of interest to Babycakes. It was in the round thing that Babycakes found the shiny metal pockets of chocolate powder that Mommy — silly Mommy — told him he could not have.

Babycakes ate the chocolate powder. Just to show Mommy, he ate his powder, shiny pockets and all.

Soon a dreadful thing happened. He had been going about his life as usual, grooming his beautiful gold self, when his entire body was overwhelmed by painful, agonizing spasms and Babycakes coughed and gagged until his fur came through his nose! He very nearly turned inside out! Nothing like this had ever happened to Babycakes before, and he was so shocked and astounded he had to go take a nap.

But someone had put fire in Babycakes' belly, and it burned and burned. Someone had stuck several Ping-Pong balls in Babycakes' belly and they bounced and bounced. Babycakes was a very unhappy cat.

Mommy rose from her platform to go to her litter room and stepped on a small, wet wad of Babycakes' used fur, and she became very unhappy, too.

She put Babycakes in a box and took him to Jennifer Needles.

Babycakes has never understood why Mommy likes Jennifer Needles. She *seems* like a nice Big One. She is covered with exotic and fascinating smells that suggest to Babycakes that she has some very interesting friends. Jennifer speaks to him very kindly when they meet, and she strokes his fine fur, and she talks pleasantly enough to Mommy, and just when Babycakes is beginning to like her, she pokes him in the most personal of places and then sticks him with pins. This almost always when Babycakes isn't feeling well anyway, and it seems acutely unfair to him.

Twice a day for several days after they visited Jennifer Needles Mommy put Babycakes on the counter and gave him sticky, bluck-tasting white stuff out of a little glass tube. Babycakes had mixed feelings about this. He rather liked the white stuff, but it's against Feline Law to appear eager, and being aloof can be SUCH a bother.

And then one day Mommy said, in a cheerful voice that lacked sincerity, "Would you like to go see Jennifer again?"

Babycakes said, "No." He said, "No" every way he knew how to say no, and when Mommy showed him that hated box Babycakes dug Mommy as his gentle way of saying, "Mommy, LISTEN to me." Mommy said several very bad words and stuffed him into the box anyway and took him to the Place Where All Sorts of Things Are.

Mommy showed Babycakes a fur-thing that had ears way too long and a nose that twitched and just a little bitty tuft of tail Babycakes would have been ashamed to own. It smelled like dinner to him, but Mommy said, "Oh, I don't think so."

Mommy showed Babycakes a huge, bad-smelling thing that wobbled all over the place and had terrible breath and that looked into Babycakes' very own box at him and said, "Woof."

Babycakes said, "Oh, I don't think so."

And then Jennifer Needles came to Babycakes' box and she pulled him out of his box, and Babycakes said, "No" to Jennifer Needles.

"Did he just hiss at you?" Mommy asked.

"Oh, it was just a little hiss," said Jennifer Needles, and she began to feel Babycakes all over his body. She felt his tummy. She felt his teeth. She looked in his ears, she played with his coat, she deliberately and intentionally made all of his hairs go the wrong way.

This was the very last straw. Babycakes said, "No" to Jennifer Needles.

"Amazing," Mommy said to Jennifer Needles. "He's NEVER hissed at me — he usually just swats me and rips off some hide."

"I think he's okay," Jennifer Needles said, and put Babycakes back in his box.

Babycakes lay very flat in his box. If anyone had looked in there they might have seen a fine gold rug. All the way home Babycakes was very quiet and very flat. Had his life been just a little different, he might have been a Persian rug. He might have learned to fly, and he might have flown far, far away from Mommy and her evil friend, Jennifer Needles.

"So," Mommy said as they rode home, just Mommy and a beautiful non-Persian gold rug, "I guess we won't be eating any more tin foil, eh, Babycakes?"

Mommy seemed inordinately pleased with herself.

training day

This morning the parking lot
was full of unusually stupid birds
—loud, arrogant birds who stood
at my wheels and demanded food
as if someone had waited on them
their entire lives. Welfare birds
(it is the welfare parking lot).
A darker, fuller bird fluttered
around them as if to say, "FLY,
you fools—fly away!"
And I sat there in my twelve-year-old
land yacht dripping antifreeze
on the pavement while baby birds
shrieked and made demands and fought
among themselves and finally scurried
off after their mothersource, never once
seeing me as anything but a missed meal.

the epidemic

just after the close of World War II an epidemic struck this country. In the next ten years, American parents, amazed that they had won the war, produced the biggest single generation of children ever born in the same decade. But they did not do so without threat. By the time I came along in 1949 parents had steeled themselves against the single most overwhelming disease ever to face an affluent society. Kids my age could also die of polio, viral pneumonia, or the flu, but the infirmity that struck the deepest terror into a parental heart was the Big Head.

Just about anything could cause the Big Head. Winning. Not coming in last. Coming in last, but coming in at all when no one expected you to finish. Doing something well, receiving a compliment, feeling good about something you did—all of this was the devil's own workshop for the Big Head. It could strike at any time, anywhere a small child had a moment of rampant ego gratification, and my parents—and the parents of all of my friends—were determined that it would never happen to a child of theirs.

If I did something well, my mother assured me it was "about time," or she told me how much better she had done with less effort at an earlier age. When other people complimented me for something she would roll her eyes and say under her breath, "Don't let it go to your head." I presumed from a very early age that nothing I would ever do would much impress my mother: I was doomed to failure, I knew, and the very BEST I could hope for would be to blend in invisibly with the rest of the losers. My mother, by comparison, had taught herself to read while gazing at billboards through her mother's womb.

I was her first child. Lovingly she shared my baby stories with me. I was born a month premature with no fingernails, no eyebrows, no baby fat, and I was bright red. My ancestors, gathered around me to welcome me into the fold, choked on phrases like "she's beautiful." I was the ugliest newborn ever presented to either branch of my family tree. This reception apparently worked on my delicate nerves and I retaliated by getting colic and screaming for the first six months of my life. In retrospect, given the opportunity to make amends I might have handled that situation differently, but I have often sensed that the tone of my relationship with my mother was set before I had much opportunity to tinker with the effects of my input.

Being her first attempt, I was particularly vulnerable to wind shifts, predators, and things that go bump in the night. My mother believed I strolled obliviously through life with my heart on my sleeve and my brains tucked firmly in my back pocket. And while it is true that I rode my bike around our P-shaped drive while wearing a hat that fell down over my eyes, allowing me to ride head-first into her parked Buick, I think her assessment was unfair and unkind. The world, in my mother's eyes—and therefore, in mine—was one endless parking lot filled with Buicks.

My childhood would have made a lot more sense if I had watched my little sister the Wee One produce her first child BEFORE I had to deal with my own mother. One day the Wee One was a pregnant woman expecting a normal baby: she gave birth, flapped her cape, and out jumped HyperMom. She had given birth to the Perfect Child and she was not worthy. Twinkies and their ilk— the mainstay of the Peck family diet—were banned on the spot: he was to dine solely on vegan fare. He would be touched only by those who had spent seventy-two days in a hermetically sealed antibiotic chamber. He could never wear yellow because it would adversely affect his emotional development, and he would never be spanked, paddled, scowled at, or otherwise physically abused. I once accidentally spoke loudly in a room where he was sleeping and she glared at me as if I had offered him a vial of heroin.

My mother was much like that when I was a child, but it never occurred to me that she might be temporarily insane, and of course it never occurs to a child that mothering is a learned art. She referred to me from time to time as her "practice piece," causing me to retreat to the gravel pit and mutter about mothers who needed more practice—but I didn't *get* it. I assumed, since I was the one getting yelled at, that it was somehow my *fault* the world was a dark and dangerous place. She present-ed such a confident and self-assured front, I just assumed there had always been rules.

I had all kinds of nonsensical rules to follow. I was told repeatedly not to get into cars with strangers — even when the strangers *insisted* I get in the car right now and be taken home. Even when I had miles to walk up and down snow-covered mountains in the dead of a Wyoming winter . . . I lived in Michigan and we had no mountains and I barely left the house in the dead of winter, but I tested all of the variables just the same. ("What if we're in a plane crash in the Andes mountains and all of our legs and arms are broken and this man stops to offer us a ride . . . ?") I was forbidden to take candy from strangers, as if hordes of candy-pushing strangers attacked me every day. (I never saw *one*. I was particularly fond of candy, so I was eager to have my mettle tested. I had a hard enough time getting my *friends* to offer me candy.) I had to watch out all of the time for people sneaking around behind me, jumping out of the bushes to give me compliments and trick me into getting the Big Head.

I remember once I asked her, "Mom — am I beautiful?" And she laughed and said, "God, no — whatever gave you *that* idea?" She died when I was twenty-seven, but I cleverly memorized all of those Mothertapes and I can play them back whenever they might be the most harmful to my emotional serenity. I have, over the course of my lifetime, completely revised my concept of the word "beautiful," but if you told me today that I am a beautiful person I would say, "Yeah, right." You can't trick me.

My mother raised me to believe that I should go quietly through life, striving to do the best I could do while keeping a low profile. If I excelled at something, other people would notice. Other people would draw attention to my skills and abilities. Other people would reward me. I should incessantly strive to please every passing stranger on the street is the lesson I learned, but my mind has always run to the extremes. Other people would let me know when I had done well—there was no reason to wander around begging for compliments.

She also raised me to believe that I was, indeed, special. There were five of us, and we were all raised to believe we were special. We were Eloise's children. We had the ability to be anything we wanted to be. We were destined for something wonderful.

We had no idea what that "something wonderful" might be and we couldn't take compliments worth beans, but . . .

I don't know how she did that. On my more bitter days, I profess not to know why a parent would raise their child to believe that drawing attention to her skills and abilities is a social crime. But I do. In my heart I am a Midwesterner, and my people live by three simple rules: work hard; wait for your turn; if you feel the need to talk about something, go plow a field until the need passes. And I don't know how you stomp on a child's ego on a regular basis and still teach that child to believe he/she has a special entitlement. Particularly when that child, as an adult, has no idea what that entitlement is, or what their "special" quality might have been.

My siblings and I have discussed this at great length during our lives. It is not something I imagined, because all three of us girls have found the same beast breathing hotly down our necks. We were supposed to have been

Special. We should have accomplished Something. We should have done something Astonishing and Wonderful and something that had never been done before. I write to feed that beast. I have also failed spectacularly, challenging the outer limits of failure, just to get her off my back. All three of us have come to see Mother's legacy as an amazing feat—and something of a family curse.

Proudly I can admit before you all that I have never suffered from the Big Head. In my fifties I have more or less conquered paralyzing attacks of worthlessness and self-doubt, but it is unlikely I will ever succumb to excessive ego. There have been times in my life when I knew, in my heart, that I was the one person in the room with the skills and talents to solve a particular problem. And I have waited patiently for the other people to recognize those skills and talents—knowing that they won't. And I have allowed that opportunity to pass because My Mother Told Me not to praise myself. And I have kicked myself in the ass for doing it. And, knowing better—I have done it again.

Nor have I taken upon myself the burden of instructing the next generations. There is nothing like a small child, wallowing in the amazing global egocentrism they enjoy, to bring my mother running to the fore, her heel raised and poised for the delicate meat of the ego. *"It's for her own good,"* she whispers insistently in my ear. *"Are you going to allow that child to wander free in this world that naked and unable to defend herself? Better you should crush her soul than let some total stranger do it later . . ."*

I paint terrible images of my mother. We had a complex relationship, my mother and I, but I never doubted that she loved me, and I never doubted that whatever she did, she did with my best interests at heart. She was afraid. She had dared to dream for herself and that dream lay half-formed and stillborn in her heart, and she wanted that not to happen to her children. She may have read the manual on child-raising in something of a hurry, and she left—me, at least—with the lifelong message I carry in my own heart. *You'll never amount to a hill of beans—but you'll be a wonderful,* special *hill of beans.*

I'll be a hill of beans with a Big Head.

sperm

i've been thinking about sperm lately.

My Beloved was telling me about friends of hers—both women—who decided to have a baby and as a result, they "spent a small fortune on sperm."

I always assumed it was free. Pretty much a by-product.

They obviously had never talked to my mother, who assured me with undaunted certainty that any man I would ever meet would willingly, happily, even eagerly give me all of the sperm I could ever hope for absolutely free of charge: that in fact most, if not all, men would *insist* on bestowing this gift. Further, *my* mother told me it was my duty to resist this generosity with every fiber of my being, which, being the good daughter that I am, I have done. I have led a nearly sperm-free life. My mother, on the other hand, presented me with four younger brothers and sisters, which suggest to me that she was made of much weaker fiber than I am.

I am assuming that all five withdrawals my mother made came from the same sperm bank. We share a number of characteristics, my siblings and I. None of us can breathe through our noses, although they appear perfectly normal on the outside (a lucky gene-stroke there: on the far side of our pool are beaks best suited for wading birds). We all have tiny little mouths full of crowded, semi-crooked teeth. We lean toward tall, and as we age, we spread out sideways. Often amply. We are not a small generation. If you were to talk to the friends of any of the five of us, it would not take long for the conversation to turn to our quirky sense of humor. So my people are tall, husky, tiny-mouthed, crooked-teethed mumblers with chronic sinus infections and a very droll way of looking at life.

But if she had *paid* for her sperm . . .

My mother liked pretty people. Thin, pretty people. Thin, pretty people with big, white, straight teeth. She yelled at me her entire life for mumbling, so I will assume she liked thin, pretty people with big, white, straight teeth and good diction. This would involve some alteration of the genetic Peck nose, which stuffs up far too often. So if she had paid for sperm, my mother would have made her withdrawals from the Aquiline Nordic Bank of Dental Excellence. Her daughters would all look like Brooke Shields. (Although none of them would ever have seen, much less starred in, *Pretty Baby.*) And, of course, we would have been brilliant. Intelligence was important to my mother. And obedience, so perhaps she would have used a German branch of the bank. Except Germans tend toward stoutness . . .

Obviously the purchase of sperm is not something to be taken lightly. Given freely is it robed and romanticized in the wanted/unwanted traits of one's loved one; stripped naked and sold like a slave on the block, it becomes a whole other entity. A shopping bag of potential characteristics. If you were to have the Perfect Child (has anyone aimed for anything less?) exactly what characteristics would you stack in his/her deck? Curly hair? Straight teeth? A Mensa IQ? The ability to lie really, *really* well? A smattering of conscience, or a good-sized dollop? Greed seeps swiftly into play. How *many* really positive characteristics would you give this Perfect Child, if you had the power to do so? I have any number of friends who have more sperm than they know what to do with, but they also have more hair on their bellies than on their heads and one or two of them are night-blind. It's possible someone even loves them, but if it were purely a matter of commerce . . .

Then there is that proprietary thing. When I was a child my uncle produced three children, divorced (intake breath sharply here) their mother, and was forced to move to the Badlands of Indiana to avoid having every cent he ever made sucked out of his pocket by the friend of the court. My grandmother (his mother) suffered endlessly over his exile, caused, she determined, in equal parts by his very poor choice in wives and his very poor taste in ex-wives. All through my childhood I guarded my pocketbook whenever That Woman came around, lest she go after my fortune as well, and year after year we enjoyed the seasonal suspense of Well Is He Coming Home for Christmas or Not? My mother was nowhere near as sympathetic. She called him cold, harsh things like "irresponsible." She was certainly in the minority. In the wisdom of my youth I perceived her attitude to be that of a bitter youngest child, a phenomenon I was only too familiar with among my own lesser siblings. There was, as I recall, no strong sense that they were his children or that his responsibility to provide for them might outlive his fondness for their mother. Times have certainly changed. Men who follow their compass wherever it leads them, leaving a trail of unsupported offspring in their wake, have become "deadbeat dads," and there is now a movement to support men in their endeavors to become permanently and irrevocably linked to whatever fruition their seeds may come to. Paternity has become fashionable.

So my assumption that the pot should cost considerably more than the seed to grow in it may no longer be accurate. Unencumbered seeds have become dear. Have a child, and you may have his father hanging around underfoot forever. (This also flies in the face of any advice provided by my mother. She harped heavily on some homily about giving away milk and then discovering you can't sell the cow.) So it would appear that just about the time women have started making real progress figuring out ways to live without grown-up little boys, the little boys have decided to grow up and not be lived without.

Which is annoying for lesbian couples.

So my Beloved's friends paid for sperm. Fatherless sperm. Clinically homeless sperm.

99.44% pure sperm.

I can hear my mother muttering.

i never had children. I grew up on a steady litany of what the ever-growing collection of children complicating my parents' marriage did to their budget, their plans for the future, and their peace of mind. What I learned from my mother is that children are expensive, ungrateful, and cut fierce holes in a toy budget. I myself could have had more and better toys had I had fewer siblings. I'm fairly sure that was not exactly what she told me (I suspect it was the perverse result of yet another pointless conversation about the "S" word) but it did nothing to inspire sisterly love. Nor did it endear the ever-arriving lesserlings to me any more than losing my room to one of them or my personal free time to another. Perhaps she was trying to build my character. But she did tell me, and it was a lesson I never forgot. Children = unappreciated sacrifice and fewer personal toys. Myself, I like toys.

Because I never had children, I have no idea how math is beaten into the skulls of inquiring young minds these days. My mother did it with a pencil, endless sheets of paper, and a stove timer.

I went to school to learn to read. I had wanted to be able to read for a long time. I spent hours on the couch in the living room with the unpictured pages of *Reader's*

Digest in my lap, practicing reading. I had no idea what the pages said so I made up the stories as I went along, but I felt very important sitting there, reading. My goal, from the day I entered school, was to read faster, better, and more accurately than anyone else in my class. I was driven to read.

I was willing to tolerate the occasional invasion of numbers in my exploration of the alphabet, but somewhere around third grade the teachers began devoting entire classes to the addition, subtraction, and later multiplication and division of numbers. I lost all interest in the project. I knew three numbers: enough, not enough, and too many. Much beyond that numbers were just annoying.

It was at this point that my teacher—a woman I had grown to love and trust—decided to involve my mother in my education. Now, my mother was a wonderful and very funny woman whom I loved with all of my heart, but I was her test child and she believed—or wanted to believe—that I was as close as flesh and bone can come to perfect. I remember being carried out of the hospital in her arms while she nervously listed all of the attributes I should aspire to. "You're going to be smart," she lectured, "and beautiful and graceful and—smart—and you're going to do very well in school and you're going to grow up to do something that will change the world. And you'll be smart . . ."

I did not fully comprehend this at the time, but almost all adults are actually better at math than most children. My mother, born, raised, and a full-grown adult before the invention of the calculator, could add, subtract, multiply, and divide in her head. Almost instantly.

I would come home from school, free at last, to find my mother waiting for me in the kitchen with sheets of multiplication problems and the stove timer. "You'll get this in no time," she would assure me, "it's really easy." And she would shove a page of math problems in front of me and set the timer. And she would sit down at the end of the table. And watch me. While the stove timer clicked off the last remaining seconds in which I might still find favor in my mother's eyes.

We did 1 through 10 plus 1 through 10 this way.

We did 1 through 10 minus 1 through 10 this way.

We did 1 through 10 times 1 through 10 this way.

By the time we came to 1 through 10 divided by 1 through 10 she had my father construct fencing from the bus stop to the back porch not altogether unlike the runs they build for cows being sent to slaughter. "You just need to *concentrate*," she would insist, as if I were deliberately being stupid just to make her look bad.

I came to dread going home. I came to hate getting off the bus. I began to see my whole life spreading out ahead of me as one hopeless morass of unsolved and unsolvable math problems ticking away like Armageddon.

"You *know* that 6 times 9 is exactly the same as 9 times 6," she would remind me as if this were perfectly evident to everyone.

The only thing that was evident to me was that when my mother shoved a pencil in my hand and set loose the timer, my mind turned to mush and the pulse behind my eyes that blurred my vision beat nervously to the same rhythm as the stove clock. All I could hear was noise, all I could see were vague shapes, and all I could think was, "You're going to fail, you're going to fail, you're going to fail . . ." and this mantra would eventually also fall into the rhythm of the timer, "You'regoing tofail, you'regoing tofail, you'regoing tofail . . ."

Inevitably I wound up crying. Sobbing, as if I were enduring some form of child abuse, and my mother, who had sacrificed all of her toys and her future to raising this tragically flawed child, would struggle to keep her composure. "It's not that *hard*," she would stress, which I heard as, *Just how stupid can one child be?*

My mother died when I was a young adult. There are times in my life when I would like to have a cup of coffee with her somewhere, just my mom and me. I would like to swap stories with her about where we've been and what we've done with our lives. She was the storyteller of her generation: there are so many things that happened when I wasn't paying attention that she would remember. *Where were we that day? What were we doing? How did that happen?* I'd like to smile and hand her the bill and watch her divide out our bills and calculate a 15 percent tip.

luna

in the late '90s a young woman climbed a California
sequoia tree and lived in the branches for over a year to
prevent the woodcutters from chopping the tree down.
She refers to the tree as Luna.

One has to wonder what Luna thought
with this oversized creature cradled
in her limbs, scurrying squirrel-like
from one branch to another
never leaving their embrace
for over a year.
What is a year to a sequoia?
Those wiser than I am say that
plants move, appearing and disappearing
to and from the places they are needed,
shifting and traversing times and spaces
unknowable to us. They are the healers
of the planet, placing salve on her burns
and laying their complex, ever-shifting hands
on her battered flesh, always moving, always
changing. Some say the planet itself,
every molecule, every germ, is a living, breathing
thing that grows and stretches and

contracts, each species living in an open,
knowing balance with every other.
Except perhaps for us
the upstarts
the rude, self-centered youngsters
who believe we alone can save the earth
who has been saving herself
for hundreds of thousands of years
and who still may find she needs to save
herself from us.

dragonflies

when i was a small child my mother took care of the babies while—particularly on weekends—my care and amusement often fell to my father. My father liked to fish. I may have set my internal alarm for zero-dark-thirty and planted myself between him and his boat, or he may have dragged me, yawning and muttering about breakfast, out of bed and into the morning air, I don't remember which. What I do remember is shoving off in the boat so early in the morning that the sounds of wood sliding across water seemed a violation of the quiet. And I remember never knowing for sure whether my father was going to actually jump into the boat at the last second, or just shove the boat and me across the lake and on into a rudderless wilderness. I was a child who always had something to worry about.

My father did not talk much. This is not a trait I inherited, particularly as a child. I was probably about this same age when I went to a movie and sat between my parents while Cyd Charisse slid down some male dancer's outstretched leg and I said, "Mommy, wouldn't you like Daddy to do that to you?" I had one of those charming little girls' voices that carried for miles with crystal clarity and that could sometimes peel paint off metal car doors. For years after that my mother used this story as an example of why I was left home with babysitters whenever my parents went out.

My father particularly did not talk while he was fishing. He told me fish could hear, and the sounds of our voices would frighten them away. (I believed this for years.) So we would reach our spot on the lake, he would throw out the anchor, set up my pole, set up his own pole, and we would sit there on the hard wooden benches of a wooden rowboat while my father went away somewhere in his head.

I believe he meditated. I believe he meditated on exactly how one man who liked to fish by himself for hours on end came to father three children—all girls—in five years. Perhaps not. I have almost never known what my father was thinking because, as I mentioned, he never talked much.

Pole fishing is not an exciting sport when you are four. A variety of things can happen—ideally a fish will bite your hook—but, all things considered, this is relatively rare. The wind can blow against your line, giving you the sense that something is nibbling from the depths below, or waves can float soundlessly across the lake and bob your bobber, giving you the illusion of imminent capture. Whatever it is that floats on the bottom of the lake and makes the water look black will move or stretch from time to time. Frogs will catapult off the shore, often issuing a short croak as they do so—this livens up pole fishing for a second or two. Turtles will slide off old logs and plop into the water, or sometimes they will just float up from the bottom and just hang in liquid suspension, only the tips of their snouts breaking the surface.

On very rare occasions a stately great blue heron will stalk suspiciously along the shoreline, eyeing the water, and freeze when he sees you. Red-winged blackbirds go about their nest-building and family-raising in the bull-rushes in spite of your presence. Every now and then one will tip his head back and trill his "oka-lee" for you.

Once in a while a snake will slide into the water and *S* his way across, exactly the same path he swims on land.

On a very good day, a dragonfly will land on the end of your pole.

Dragonflies are flexible sticks with two sets of amaz-ing, translucent wings and one set of big, shiny eyes. They have three sets of feet that they use to continually position themselves. My favorite dragonflies are blue, but they also come in green and in an amazing array of sizes and colors and shapes. I did not know this as a child, but dragonflies are some of the oldest life forms on the planet. They were here before the dinosaurs and they are still here, although it remains to be seen if they can survive mankind. Like everything else that does not thrive in strip malls and land-fills, they are losing their habitat to us, which is ironic, given that it is their very adaptability that has allowed them to survive as long as they have. But I didn't know that as a kid. I knew two facts about dragonflies (although perhaps not when I was five). They only live twenty-four hours and they do nothing but have sex. Neither fact is true. They are voracious eaters and some of them live for months and sometimes years. Nonetheless, I would hardly be the first person to idolize something for reasons that have nothing to do with its real nature.

I loved them because one dragonfly would attach itself to my pole or even more interesting, to my line — and sit there being exotic and blue and giant-eyed, quivering on the nearly invisible line over the water. They seemed to me to be like fairies, beautiful and exotic and utterly uninterested in me. I could get lost in the study of a dragonfly wing. They were a weightless latticework of black frame and iridescent surface, like the skins of soap bubbles. Sooner or later another dragonfly just like the first would come along and land on top of it. And then they would begin to dance. They would roll themselves into wheels and the letter P and sometimes they would even fly away as my last initial in the wind.

"*Daddy*," I would whisper, remembering not to wake the fish. "Daddy—what are they *doing*?" I don't remember that I required an answer. I may have intuitively known, or perhaps just the wonder of it amazed me and I wanted him to see.

The answer was always the same. He would look up, and he would study the dragonflies a moment, and then he would say very Dad-like, "Watch your bobber."

(fat girls and estrogen patches)

the three of us are riding together in the car, our coats shrugged up against the cold, when Rae rolls her eyes, savagely winds down her window, and throws her head into the breeze like the family dog. Of all of the indignities that age has inflicted upon us in our combined 150 years, the inability to maintain a stable body temperature has been for me the most annoying. When they dragged me out of fifth grade to attend a lecture on "Our Changing Bodies" nobody told me that the only process longer and less charming than Becoming a Woman would be the Unbecoming. I have lost my sense of humor more than once.

I was a fairly even-tempered child before my hormones kicked in. No one noticed because I was evenly morose and brooding, but the fact remains that hysteria does not run in my family until, like fine wine, we begin to ferment. I woke up one morning with the incontrovertible knowledge that everyone in the known universe hated me, that both of my parents should probably die of sheer stupidity, that the basic definition of the word "awful" was my personal life. I remember raging at my math teacher because he did not advance me to the "gifted" math class—not because I cared a whit about math or could even add two and two—but because all of my friends were in the gifted math class and he was single handedly destroying my social life. I almost never slept all through high school because my body was humming like a tuning fork and would not stop. I threw things, I screamed, I said horrible things to my mother, and I spent three days out of every month curled up in the fetal position around a hot water bottle or sprawled out on my back with an ice pack on my head. My entire family came to see these days as blessed relief.

Sherry is having cramps again—she's gone to her room.

Oh, thank God.

Compared to my friends, I did not have a particularly difficult passage into womanhood. Gradually my life calmed down, my moods leveled out, and my siblings began to lose that *is she Loretta Young or Hannibal Lecter today?* look in their eyes. (Or, since I was the oldest of all of us and three out of five of us were girls, I gradually became the least of their problems.) I had friends who turned pale and passed out on certain days of the month, I had friends who were debilitated by cramps and had to be shot up with muscle relaxers (not unlike aging race-horses) to get through the day. By my early thirties I had become so mellow that I remember listening to my women friends talk about PMS as I had once listened to friends describing the effects of smoking pot—something I had heard a great deal about, but almost never experienced personally.

In my mind I am still in my early thirties. When I say that, some women snort and mutter, "Yeah, right," but they're upstarts. Ambitious weeds in a field of old, established daisies. They still imagine that there is some time in their lives when they will feel like "adults," when the occasional disfavor blessed on them by their parents will no longer faze them, when any situation that presents itself to them will have a clear and apparent solution. We won't tell them the truth—it would be like telling them the ending of the book they are reading.

I grew older. More seasoned. Stable. I moved on into my forties a woman of calm disposition, a woman who had battled demons in her youth and if she had not won, she had at least broken even. And then one day my supervisor suggested I redo something I had already finished and I contemplated killing him. In fact, there was almost no contemplation to it: I exploded in a lava flow of fury and vitriol so intense the man literally dropped to the floor and belly-crawled to safety. I stood there, shaking with rage while this small, invisible child who is my conscience tugged gently at my symbolic skirt and murmured, *It's not all THAT, you know . . .*

Beyond the occasional homicidal rage, I got out lucky. My Beloved, spurred on by the pathetic cries from her coworkers—*more yam cream, more yam cream*—tried hormone replacement therapy—which worked flawlessly for me—and developed such intense pain in her legs that she was virtually on crutches for a while. According to her doctor hormone therapy cannot produce the sort of symptomology she was displaying, although it began shortly after she began HRT and it ended shortly after she ended HRT. Her sister, who had a hysterectomy in her early twenties, endured years without estrogen in her system at all until her doctor put her on estrogen therapy:

and then she developed breast cancer and he jerked her back off. In fact the whole question of HRT is a *Sophie's Choice* of options: would you rather bet against cancer or heart disease? Is your physical comfort and sense of well-being worth genetically mutating all of the fish bred within your closed water system? Ten years ago HRT was judged "harmless." Now that I've taken it for five years, doctors aren't so sure. It "may" not be as effective as doctors once believed it to be. It "may" have more serious side effects than previously believed.

My father's mother, who would not have acknowledged anything so earthy as her change of life, told me about bouts of near-suicidal depression in her mid-forties. She told me about being taken to the doctor who injected her with massive shots of vitamin B_{12} that left her wired and anxious and sobbing for no apparent reason. She was a woman who preferred to think of herself as a sort of ethereal spirit temporarily bound to a corporate form, the care of and needs of which were not the things that "ladies" discussed, so how much of her illness during this time was her life and how much of it was her change I have no way of knowing. Still, while she was always vulnerable to seasonal affective disorder, she appeared never to be as susceptible to paralyzing depressions in her later years as she was during her late forties and early fifties.

I've noticed lately that my sisters, who followed me fearlessly into puberty, are now showing signs of having tagged along too closely across the next great chasm. We would be the three women standing on the front porch in twenty-degree weather fanning ourselves. None of us currently own a decent winter coat—we've just never gotten

round to buying one here lately. We amuse each other with
stories about waking up at three o'clock in the morning and
pitching all of the blankets off the bed, only to wake up later
cold and curse the gremlins in the thermostat.

I lost my mind in the battle of the hormones. I joke
that it probably fell out with all of the hair that was leaving my head at the time—or perhaps it was simply
bleached colorless during the War Against the Gray. My
bush acquired the same spindly legginess of an aging
spirea. All of that missing hair and more sprouted immediately out of my chin, thicker, bolder, more resistent to
styling and shaping than it had ever been before. But the
thing I have come to miss most is the English language.
I used to speak in full sentences. People used to enjoy listening to me as I told stories or recalled past events. I
was funny. I was charming. I was not perpetually saying,
"Oh, that . . . *thing*, you know—my friend what's-her-
name used to have one . . ."

Women older than I am assure me I will eventually
recover my ability to use more than three words sequen-
tially. I have doubted them in the past—sometimes it has
seemed that I will never spontaneously remember a noun
or a verb any more specific than "umm . . ." But there
have been other predictions I brushed aside as being too
improbable as well. For instance, I never thought I could
ever feel this way again, I felt this experience was dead to
me, washed away in the torrents of time, but yesterday a
peculiar and persistent feeling came over me, seeping into
my awareness, waking long-dead memories of younger,
happier days. I had to think about it for some time, but
eventually I identified this feeling: I was cold.

puppy love

when i was a freshman in high school I became the light in a young man's eyes. I was oblivious to my own charms or their effects on others, and he was too shy to approach me. We were, I believe, attending a parade in downtown Coldwater when, utterly by accident, his family found themselves standing next to mine, and his mother told my mother that her son had a crush on me. I was dumbfounded, because I'd had no recollection of ever having seen the boy before.

Nonetheless, galvanized by his mother's proclamation of his affections, he began seeking me out and involving me in awkward and self-conscious conversation. He made a point of being at my locker every morning about the time I got off the bus and he walked me to my first class.

We were seen.

One of the more popular girls in school, who had never had much reason to acknowledge me before, walked up to me and said, "I saw you walking in the hall today with your boyfriend while I was walking with mine." Obviously I had taken the first step toward social acceptance.

I was never the belle of the ninth grade. While many

of the boys were still growing, I had achieved my full
height three years before they would. Nor was I ever
slender. I had common mouse-brown hair that was baby-
fine and prone to oiliness and that was never, never
intended for the huge, poofy dos of the mid-sixties. I
worked much harder at it then—albeit intermittently—
but I wore it pretty much the way I wear it today, the difference being that now it just does what it wants to do,
and when I was in ninth grade, it did what it wanted to
do in spite of my best efforts to make it do something
else. I had acne. I had a precocious vocabulary for a
child my age and I had a reputation for reading everything and anything. Most of my peers assumed I was
much smarter and academically more accomplished than
I felt. My mother had told me I would never get a boy on
looks so I had best work on my personality, but she had
any number of complaints about my personality as well,
so I had decided my only possible avenue of success was
to wow the world with my intellect.

One gauge of this intellect might be that I believed,
far past the ninth grade, that the way to impress a boy
was to outsmart him.

I hardly ever dated.

My boyfriend—as almost everyone but me had come
to think of him—was a six-foot redhead with acne and a
dismal grade point average. He was a very nice boy. He
was altogether taken with me.

I had power over him.

I could get him to do things for me.

If nothing else, his presence reminded everyone who
saw us that *someone* wanted me.

I just didn't want it to be him.

He embarrassed me. He was big and ungainly and seriously besotted.

And boring.

I kept telling myself that eventually I would learn to enjoy conversations with him, but I rapidly reached the point where I felt a little ripple of *oh, shit* pass through me every time I saw him coming. I spent what seemed like hours gazing with frozen fascination into his face, but all I ever saw was a very sweet boy I was going to have to hurt to ditch.

I felt horrible the whole time I walked the halls with him. I felt dishonest. I felt like I was using him to gain something for myself, and I resented him because I wasn't gaining anything worthwhile. And I was angry because I kept hoping he would discover I was significantly less wonderful than he thought I was and he never seemed to notice, which meant I was going to have to either die of boredom or break his heart.

I broke his heart.

I can still remember the expression on his face when I told him I didn't want to walk the halls with him anymore.

I felt like I had just stomped a puppy.

To this day I remember two things from this experience: (1) how incredibly awful I felt because I could not like him back the way he liked me, and (2) that he was going steady with another girl three weeks after I dumped him. They used to walk the halls together. If she saw me, she would reach out and gently take his hand.

the tyranny of trees

despite my parents' best efforts, I still tend to look at work much the way I look at a novel: it should have a beginning, a middle, and an end. The end of work has always been of keen interest to me. How long will this take? When will we be done? When does this *end*? When I think about my father I think about those cold, crisp days of early spring when mud puddles are mushy and sharp, filled with melting crystals of ice, and there is the faint smell of leaves burning somewhere in the air. In my memory I am too small to keep up with him, so I am standing abandoned somewhere in the yard while he patrols his lawn, picking up fallen tree limbs, checking for mole damage and dead spots and winter ruts. We will be outside working all day until our noses run and our cheeks are red and when we finally come inside we will suddenly get cold and shiver for a long time before we warm up again.

When my parents bought the house where I grew up there were as many as six elm trees in the yard—big trees, in my memory at least, and old. And dead. Dutch elm disease had either just come through or came through just after we moved there. Whatever the timing, we spent the first few years we lived there cutting down elm trees, cutting up elm trees, hauling away elm trees, digging out the stumps of elm trees. There was also a fencerow around the garden that was filled with seedling trees, and there was a rough sort of junkyard behind the foundation of the old gas station where weedling trees like ash and poplar and self-seeding maple had grown up. We tore those all out. We hauled away all of the rocks and the trash and the broken glass from the junk-yard. When we finished these projects my father's lawn spread from the driveway to the gravel pit on the left side of the house to the fenceline just short of the pond on the right side and all of it was smooth and level and kept in neatly trimmed grass. We lived in a park.

For the first ten years we lived there my parents fought about trees. My mother questioned why they had even bought the property if my father intended to cut down "every tree in the yard." My father classified trees according to their habits. There were "goddamned trees" like the walnuts that dropped bumper crops of hard green balls all over the lawn, choking the mower and eventually turning brown and staining everything they touched a dark mahogany that never comes out. We had a metal roof on the garage and every time the wind blew in the fall we could hear the walnuts drop like distant artillery. There were "those dirty trees" like the willows that dropped a sixth of their growth on his freshly man-icured lawn every time the wind blew. There were the fruit trees—two pear trees, three apple trees—that lobbed rotting fruit all over the property. There was actually only one pear tree, but it had been grafted to grow two distinctly different kinds of pears. There were the big mushy yellow pears that fell on the ground and attracted bumblebees so that small children, banished to the yard to pick up pears, were always in mortal peril of being stung to death and carried away. There were the small, hard green pears, which only rotted on the bottom and thus made our hands sticky and yucky. We all hate pears. I hated picking up rotten apples, too, but we used the apples in our own baking and canning. We made particularly appealing jars of mud, peeled concord grapes (they looked like eyeballs), and little green apples that we presented to our mother every fall.

We all worked very hard to trim back the encroaching wilderness and make our yard our home. We owned seven-eighths of an acre and we push-mowed an acre and a half. We mowed the property behind our yard that leads up to the big pond. We mowed the little woods to the right of our yard and both sides of the driveway into the gravel pit behind our house. We mowed the grass in the ditch a quarter of a mile down the road in either direction. If it was green and it grew we mowed it. When my father fired up his mowing machine, neighbors all up and down the road jumped up to countermow their perimeters. My father was the gold standard in lawn-care.

There was a time when I could have told you exactly how many trips with a 22-inch mower every section of that lawn required. And every year an adjoining blade of grass fell over onto our lawn and that too had to be cut and became a part of the weekly mow. My father eventually bought a riding mower, and some lesser sibling inherited lawn duty just when it could have been fun because I apparently took up too much space making turns. This defect has not handicapped me in my adult life.

We had cut down all of the trees my mother had not lashed herself to like some kind of demented Californian. "The spirit of the trees has chained herself to the walnut grove again," I would advise my father, and he would just nod, surrounded as he was by crazywomen. I was bitter, therefore, when he began showing up with puny, spindly little maple trees all jammed into paper buckets.

I believe — I can't swear to this — that there were nine of them, originally.

He loaded them all in the trailer behind our tractor and took them for a ride through our park. At odd intervals he would stop, pull one off the trailer, plop it down on the ground, and step back to study it critically. He would cock his head to one side and then the other. He would walk away four feet, stop, and whirl back around as if the tree had been thinking about sneaking out of some ill-defined task. He would set the paper bucket four inches to the right of where it had been, and then eight inches to the left. Sometimes he would just rock the bucket back and forth as if he were trying to screw it into the ground.

He did this with all nine trees, until in the end he had nine spindly, weakly little maple trees in paper buckets parked all over our lawn.

"Okay," he said, and he wandered off.

"Well, that's dumb-looking," I said to my siblings.

"They're going to be hard to mow around," my siblings said to me.

"I don't like it," I agreed. "Something's up."

And indeed it was: it was my father with a shovel thrown over his shoulder. "You're going to need to get a bucket of water," he said to me.

This is the most misleading sentence my father has ever said to me, bar none. I believed, at the time I heard it, that for some unknown reason my father had determined he needed one bucket of water.

I found a bucket. I filled it with water. I hauled it four miles across the lawn to where he was.

He picked up my bucket and poured the water into a hole he had just dug. He handed the bucket back to me and looked expectant.

It took five buckets of water to plant each tree. His children were sprawled all over the lawn like spent slaves, but we had not yet heard the worst of it.

Those stupid little trees required five buckets — twenty-five *gallons* — of water apiece for the first twenty-five years of their life. It makes no difference whether you talk to me or the UnWee or the Wee One or our Little Brother or our Baby Brother, we will all tell you the same thing. Barely taller than five-gallon pails ourselves, we hauled those pails full of water five times a tree for nine trees every day, day in, day out, across mountains and deserts uphill both ways through droughts and dust storms and gale-force winds.

If you were to look at my father's lawn today you would find a beautifully manicured park filled with lush, healthy sugar maples. One was killed by lightning, another rotted in the crotch and split, but most of them are full, mature trees. Beautiful trees. Sometimes we gather in my father's lawn, and someone — a newcomer — will comment on how beautiful my father's trees are.

It doesn't matter which of us answers, it's always the same. We look at the trees, and we nod, and we mutter, "Water hogs." And one more time we tell the story of the never-ending bucket brigade.

how i came out

i was browsing through my personal poetry the other
day and I came across a particularly cranky one I wrote
to a friend who was struggling with her sexuality. My
friend had done everything she was supposed to do. She
went to college, she got married, she had two children,
she got divorced, she got a decent job, she fell in love
with a woman. Wait. Women falling in love with other
women is not on the "should" list her mother gave her.
My friend was drawn to me because I was out, I was
open about my life, and I would talk to her about the
subject that had become the all-consuming passion of her
life. I knew other gay women and I was willing to introduce her. On the other hand . . . I was out. I was open
about my life. People *knew* about me. She reminded me
of the need for discretion—at least in terms of betraying
her "secret"—about seventeen times a day, and as a
result I wrote a scathing poem to her (*"we expect more from
sisters"*) which, as far as I know, she's never read.

I felt very cool and righteous when I wrote that
poem.

Being in the throes of creative genius, I probably had
just momentarily forgotten the book I threw against the
wall on Waterman Avenue, or the two hours I spent

driving across the state to visit a bookstore so I could walk in the front door and right on out the back. Or the twenty-odd years where I lived a completely schizophrenic life with my gay friends on one stop on I-94 and my straight friends on the other. Coming out may be a process, but I had pulled my life together: she needed to shape up.

She was struggling because she had a grown child who had made vaguely homophobic remarks. Imagine letting a small thing like your offspring hold you back from being all that you can be.

This is how I came out. I have to remind myself of this from time to time because I am apt to rewrite for myself a much more courageous past than the one I lived.

I was fat, I was socially inept, I had zits, my mother told me I would never finish anything. I wanted more than anything else to be a writer and my mother told me I would starve on the street because no one wanted to read the dark and depressing melodramatic dreck I wrote. (She did not actually use the word "dreck." What she said was, "Sherry, why does everything you write have to be so dark? You have a wonderful sense of humor, why don't you show that once in a while?" She obviously had no understanding of drama.) The last thing I needed in my life was to wake up one morning a lesbian.

In fact, I was not a lesbian. I didn't even like the word. (As a sort of lingering denial, I misspelled it for years.)

No. I was a writer. I had a perpetual cast of imaginary people in my head, going about their own lives, which were always more dramatic, meaningful, and intense than mine. One day, for no obvious reason, my main imaginary character fell in love with his best friend.

Imagine that. I was so creative that I was having male-on-male sexual fantasies in my head. It had nothing to do with me, of course, because I am not male . . .

. . . But it did pique my curiosity, and I decided I needed to research the peculiar direction this character had (autonomously) taken. (Did I mention that these imaginary characters who live in my head have the bad habit of becoming just intensely, passionately fascinated by issues that six months later would become unexpected issues in my own life?) The first thing I discovered was that almost no one had ever written a book about gay men.

I went to my local bookstore, where I found two books: *Burn in Hell, Pervert* and *We All Live a Long, Long Way Away.*

I determined that perhaps the bookstore where I was shopping was too small, so I went to Ann Arbor. I went to college in Ann Arbor, where I vaguely remembered something called "gay and lesbian dances." I had always wanted to go (we have no idea why) but none of my roommates had ever agreed to go with me. Now, as it turned out, I should have gone, because I could have been doing research for my book. (For my main male character who, all of his own accord, had gone gay on me one day and started boffing his best friend. Try to keep up.)

I found a book that was a kind of travel guide for gay men. It was titled *The Gay Insider.* It was written under a pseudonym by this amazingly charming and enthusiastic young man who traveled all over the United States checking out the gay hot spots (both of them) at the time. He was funny. He was delightful. I sat right down to write him a letter. I wanted to tell him how much I enjoyed his book, how I had achieved a new understanding of the trials and tribulations of gay men, how I felt he and I had forged, through his book, a common bond, which was that he was a gay man and I was a straight woman with an imaginary male character in her head who had gone gay one day for no good reason. (Much the same way cider just turns into vinegar, I would imagine.)

That letter went to hell in a handbasket. That letter was twenty-three pages long and it was still explaining why I (of all people) read his book in the first place. The warm glow of kinship had flared up in my face and burned out, I was mad at the author, mad at myself. I was furious with my main character and his flexible sexuality that had gotten us all into this mess to begin with. I snapped, "I am NOT a lesbian," and threw the book against the wall.

I could prove it.

And I sat right down, and I wrote a concentrated, distilled, intentionally *lesbian* story. I picked out every lesbian impulse I had ever had and I exaggerated it, intensified it, threw it on the floor, and jumped on it seven times while wearing boots. I wrote a story about a *dyke*.

(I am a creative writer. I write fiction. I can write anything I want to write.)

I wrote a short story about a woman going to her best friend's wedding.

I wrote the first honest, frankly biographical short story based on my own life experiences I had ever written. The main character was in love with her best friend. She didn't *want* to be. She did everything she could to deny it, she would have died rather than admit it. But reading that story, it was remarkably clear what the conflict was. Unlike the other three times I had tried to write the same story, casting myself as a man, and the story made no sense at all.

It took me three weeks of conscious practice to use the word "lesbian" in a sentence that did not also include the word "not."

It took me six months to make a deliberate effort to meet another lesbian.

It took me twenty years to get so cool with my sexuality that I could fault a sister for asking me to deny part of my identity to protect hers.

The process of self-acceptance is never-ending. A few days ago my editor sent me a review a bookseller wrote to publicize *Fat Girls and Lawn Chairs*. The bookseller had written, "Cheryl Peck is a fat, lazy lesbian from Michigan who doesn't care who knows it . . ." I took immediate offense. I turned to Babycakes and I snapped, "How dare that man call me 'lazy'?"

walking home

i was driving home from work. I was tired. It was a cold, rainy day following too many cold, rainy days that have stood between me and a warm and welcoming spring; it was damp in the truck and slick on the highway, and as I rattled up to a busy intersection of two one-way streets, two two-way streets, and the railroad tracks, there—in the middle of this frantic man-made mess—was a dog. Probably not an old dog, but unmistakably a tired dog. A dog with sore feet and aching muscles and a slight limp. A wet, tired, lost dog who looked up at me in the middle of the road and ripped out my heart.

I had stopped for the light: I opened the truck door and tried to tempt him into my truck, but he looked at me warily and then ducked his head and padded determinedly into the path of three more lanes of traffic. And my light changed.

Frantic, I drove through the intersection and around the block, picked the wrong road back, drove in another wild circle, and ended up parked in front of the train station. Abandoning the truck, I set out on foot to find him, half expecting to find his freshly killed body on the highway. But he had made it across all three lanes and was sitting in the grass beside the road like a weary traveler who has gone as far as he can go.

I tried to walk up to him, but he dragged himself up, stared at me a minute, and then started walking again.

I called him, but he ducked his head and trudged along, keeping just about the same distance between us.

I felt awful. My imagination kept running off on riffs of what it must feel like to be lost and homeless in the middle of a world that makes no sense. I wanted to take him home (to my dog-hating cat) and give him shelter (in my cat-hair-coated home) and perhaps a decent meal (cat food?). I imagined how my life might be changed by the addition of one small (fifty-pound), bedraggled traveler. (I could give up my social life, re-home my personal dog-hating cat herd, all without ever addressing issues like housetraining, previous owner location, and where on three-fifths of an acre one keeps what looked like many parts of a golden retriever/Saint Bernard/Lab mix.)

I did give up. Although I was/am not convinced it was in his best interest, I allowed him to choose not to be adopted by me. Perhaps he went home.

Perhaps.

give me a head with hair . . .

we were waiting for our port-a-pit chickens to roast when I first saw her. I didn't pay much attention to her at first because I was hungry and I had begun to suspect that the port-a-pit chicken roasters were inexperienced in the art of port-a-pit chicken roasting and there were not enough hours left in the day for my port-a-pit chicken — for which I had already paid — to achieve anything close to the state of roastedness. I was hungry (never a good way to begin) and I was bored, because there is nothing quite like waiting for something you have already guessed you're never going to get. What brought my attention back to the little girl was the girly-girl flip of her long, luxurious hair. She would tip her head back almost like a dog being butt-scratched, and I realized she was feeling her hair flow down her back. Because it was acquired hair. A fall. She was about eight years old and someone had pinned about a four-pound ponytail to the back of her head — she was in girly-girl heaven.

About the only thing that ever appealed to me about being a girl was long hair. Long, thick, glorious hair cascading down my back if I so chose. And I did so choose. My Grandmother Molby had never cut her hair — never — and every night she would sit down at her dressing table and unbraid her hair until it hung all around her like a gossamer curtain from the top of her head to just gently touching the floor. And she would comb it. I knew that if I could just convince my mother to stop chopping mine off, people would stop saying things like, "She's . . . he's . . . a cute little thing . . ." I didn't mind being mistaken for a boy, but if I had to actually be a girl I wanted the perks that went with it. The only perk I could see was hair.

I was born bald and I stayed that way for at least two years. I had about seven strands of babyfur, which my mother painstakingly formed into two little curls on the top of my head for every photograph she had taken of me. The babyfur was blond, but when actual hair grew in to replace it, it was almost exactly the color of a well-stirred mud puddle. It was baby-fine. It grew quickly. It grew long. It almost—but never really—curled, which means it bent here and there, and about five strands of it, gathered together like a delinquent gang at the back of my part, stood straight up.

The other thing my baby-fine hairs that almost but not quite curled did, and did with a vengeance, was form tight, unforgiving wads around the base of my hairline. I didn't care: I had hair. But my mother had no patience with my nascent dreadlocks. I came to turn pale and wobble off like a belle with the vapors whenever I saw my mother coming toward me with a hairbrush, and I suppose some people might have assumed she beat me with it, which wasn't true. She brushed my hair with it. She would wind that brush through my hair, get a good, solid hold on the snarls along my neckline, and rip them out by the roots. I would shriek and scream and wail and the next thing I knew I had another bowl over my head and my mother was scissoring off all of my hair. "If you can't stand still and be quiet and get your hair combed, then you can't have long hair," she would lecture me, as if there were an obvious choice somewhere in that.

I may not have had a long, flowing mane of hair during the daytime, but at night, in my bed, I knew exactly what to do. I would slip quietly out of bed, creep up beside the UnWee's crib, and nab her baby blanket, ripping it out of her still clenching and unclenching little fingers. (I often thought she should have been a cat.) I would beat it back to my own bed, and there, in the privacy of my own fantasy, I would drape her baby blanket around my head, tie it with a scarf, and I had it: thick, thick, *thick*, long hair. It came to my waist and beyond. It weighted down my head, it flowed down my back, it was soft and . . . black, where I was (pale pink, to the untrained eye). I was a fair young maiden on a ship, flirting demurely with pirates, or an Indian princess . . . I probably would have worn my created hair to school, left to my own devices, but once again my mother stood in my way. *Get that rag off your head, Cheryl . . .*

Because there was danger that my life might have passed without trauma, the haircare industry invented home perms. "Perm" is short for "permanent," and the first home perms rivaled pestilence and disease in the damage they could inflict on a child's head. First I had to wash my hair, and then I had to rinse my hair in some chemical solution that removed its will to live. Then I was tied to uncomfortable wooden chairs in the kitchen, covered with a drop cloth, given one small handkerchief to save my eyes, and told to sit still. My mother would soak little sheets of paper in some ammonia solution, pick out four strands of my hair, wrap it in the paper, and then twirl it around little plastic bones that she secured to my head by driving them into my scalp with her thumbs. The ammonia solution would leak down my forehead toward my eyes, and my job was to mop without moving. Once all of my individual hairs were wrapped in bones, she would douse my head with yet more ammonia solution, wrap cotton around my forehead and in front of my ears to keep my face from scalding, and then she would set the stove timer.

I was not allowed to move while the solution perked on my head. I could probably have talked to my mother, had she not wandered off to do laundry or something equally boring.

When the timer went off she would come back and rinse my entire head, and then she would pour a neutralizing solution over it, which—with any luck—would stop the burning. Then she tore all of the plastic bones out of my head, sorted out the papers, and rinsed my hair some more. Even at that, as I remember I could not comb my hair or do much of anything but sit around with a towel wrapped around it for another hour or so while it "set."

In exchange, my friend could tell I'd just gotten a new perm for five days based on the smell in my hair alone.

My hair responded to a perm by not so much curling as becoming . . . crinkled . . . in texture. What it did was

frenetic and intense, but it bore only a passing resem-
blance to a "curl." Other girls I went to school with had
mothers less skilled in the art of torturing their daughters, and their hair fried. Their overpermed hair turned
brittle and lifeless in color, and often all they could do
was wait until it grew out.

I fought with my hair most of my life. I grew it long
as an adult, only to discover I didn't enjoy combing out
the snarls around my neck any more than I'd enjoyed
having my mother do it. And while each time I grew it
out I imagined that *this time* it would be thick and sleek
and my inner beauty would begin to break out . . . It
never happened. I have a great many strands of quite
fine hair, but the difference between a lot of nothing and
not much of nothing is not all that obvious. My life
became much calmer when I understood that my hair
almost always does about the same thing, and the easiest
solution was just to let it do it. I'm almost never mistak-
en for a little boy anymore anyway.

I never did get my port-a-pit chicken. It was a fund-
raiser, put on by good-hearted people trying to do something nice to support a friend. We had somewhere else
we had to be long before that overcommitted chicken
would have been done, so we let our cooks know we
were leaving, left our money as a contribution to the
cause, and went on. But I still think back fondly of that
little girl with her fine, thick, borrowed hair. It makes me
wonder wistfully whatever happened to that wonderful
blanket . . .

We sold my father's truck
(automatic transmission,
independence,
personal freedom
all standard options,
no extra cost)
because he could no longer
see well enough to drive,
and because none of us
wanted his battered reason
making decisions on the road.
Still, somewhere in my mind
there is his big black truck
with four blankets neatly folded
in the back (for padding
and hauling) and six two-by-fours
all cut exactly the right length
to stabilize the rototiller;
his little wooden box collection;
the rubber band that held his maps
the extra pair of sunglasses
perpetually thrown on the dash;

and the John Deere baseball cap
that hung in the back of the cab.
This was my father.
This *was* my father: since then
we have taken him apart,
dismantled him one piece
at a time. Discarding
the trappings of his life
to save it.

crackers

i have learned any number of things about my friends long after the fact—or, not necessarily about them, more about what they really think of me. I will be cruising along in a relationship, quite comfortably ensconced, and we will be reminiscing about the first time we met and my new, comfortable friend will laugh and say, "You know, the first time I met you, you were really being a bitch."

Imagine watching my jaw drop.

Yet, it's happened again.

I have no recollection of such bitchery. We were all to meet for dinner at my house and one contingency of the crew was (because it's tradition for lesbians) late. I am one of the few card-carrying lesbians I know who can actually sit down and calculate what I need to do before I arrive at a selected location and how long these combined tasks will take, so that my truck and I arrive at the chosen location on or just slightly before the precise clock stroke originally agreed upon. If my friends tell me to be at their house by 6 p.m., I will be there by 5:55. Ready. With gas in the tank, money in my pocket, and (and this is the bone of contention) every firm belief that my friends will be equally present and prepared to begin our adventure.

I was once identified as the weak link on a camping/
biking/stargazing trip because I lived so far away, and I
was reminded several times that I needed to arrive at the
departure location precisely at 6 p.m.—earlier if I
could—because we had miles to go and promises to
keep. I arrived at my friends' house at 5:47. One had
driven away to perform some emergency recycling, and
the other was pondering their as yet unpacked suitcase.
I'm sure those thirteen minutes made all the difference. I
spent an hour and a half sitting on the curb, whimsically
thinking about all of the wonderful last-minute emergencies I could have tended to in my own life, those mere
sixty-five miles away, had I only realized that "By six at
least—earlier if you can" meant, "Oh, give or take, about
eight."

However, the specific bitchy moment I don't even
remember and my friend has since forgiven me for
involved another crucial element that weakens my asser-
tion that she misremembered. She reminded me, *"You
were hungry."*

Don't *make* me wait to eat when I am hungry. Don't
even pull into my drive forty-five minutes after we were
supposed to leave for the restaurant without having
three flats, a broken wrist, and a heartwrenching tale
about being beaten and left as roadkill by rabid bikers to
defend your tardiness. Every time I have ever had to
wait for you before I could eat will come up. A *long*, dramatic (and not all that even-tempered) description of
why gas-pumping, cash-getting, people-picking-upping,
and errands truly are NOT negative-time components
that will allow a sixty-minute drive to remain a sixty-

minute drive . . . This will come up. The right way to plan your life so you need never inconvenience me again will come up. Friends who know me well have intimated (gently, of course) that I can lose my sense of humor when I'm hungry.

My dear friends will warn new companions, "Don't mind Cheryl—she'll calm right down after we feed her," while new companions think to themselves, *This woman is a raving bitch.*

It can happen. My sense of moral outrage can be pushed to the point that I am overcome by righteous indignation, I am galvanized by the truth of my vision, and I resort to a teaching method known as Slash and Trash. It may seem like a simple inconvenience to everyone else, but I have the depth and breadth of understanding to see how this singular disregard for my personal needs is indicative of probably fatal character flaws, flaws that need to be exorcised and cauterized by the purity of my wrath.

This may explain why so many of my friends, when they sense they may be a little late, greet me with a big grin, a warm hug, and a little package of crackers.

ferron

after the show ferron walked right past me, close enough that I could have reached out and touched her.

We had all taken time off work and piled into the good car to drive from Kalamazoo to Lansing to see her, and the trip—while conveniently beneficial for us all—was a birthday present for Rae. We listened to Ferron CDs all through the drive, and all through the drive Rae giggled like a little girl and crooned about becoming "Mrs. Ferron." All through dinner at the Tuba Museum Rae lusted after women in the restaurant, but in her heart she stayed true to Ferron. By the time we reached Creole Gallery there was nothing Rae could do but grin, and when we copped seats in the front row, right next to the stage, Rae went into a sort of misty, grinning trance. Ferron came on. Ferron sang Rae's favorite song ("Girl on a Road"). Rae's goal in life, all evening, was to have Ferron sign her T-shirt.

Rae is shy. She is not shy all of the time: she appears to succumb to sudden bouts of shyness that attack without warning, undermine her determination, and leave her standing a step or two from her goal, unable to reach it.

I can be reserved, remote, unwilling to commit, "Peckish" . . . but I am not, in comparison to Rae, shy.

So when Ferron walked past me I did not reach out and touch her: instead I said, "Could you sign my friend's T-shirt?"

And she did. She was very gracious (although, I suspect, not overwhelmingly pleased). We all told her we had enjoyed her concert, and she went on to wherever she had been going before I interrupted her.

In retrospect I would probably not make a request like that again. I made a presumption of . . . ownership, really . . . that does not exist in the real world. I assumed, since I had just spent two hours listening to her music, her stories, and her life, that there existed some sort of intimacy between us that — however real to me — is curiously one-sided. Although she moved me deeply with her work, there is really no way to adequately say that in a two- or three-minute offstage conversation while she struggles valiantly to get away from me. It is the curious relationship of a performer to her audience that when the performance is over, there are a hundred people sitting in the audience thinking, "Her life is just like mine — we have this, this, and this in common, I've felt the same exact way about that, we are bonded, Ferron and I, over this shared experience," and there is one woman on the stage thinking, "Well, at least they laughed in the right places."

She didn't know that Rae took a night off work to come see her. She didn't know the trip was a birthday gift from her friends. She didn't know that Rae loves that particular song because it speaks to her own life and leaving her family in Oklahoma. She didn't know that of all of the songs she has written, the one that speaks

almost mystically to me appears to have been written out
of an experience that echoes through my own life. She
didn't know my friend had set her goal for the evening as
getting Ferron to sign her T-shirt.

I don't know Ferron from the woman in the moon.
Until I saw her in concert, I didn't even know she was
Canadian—I thought she lived in Wyoming. And while
I presume to have all of this knowledge about her inner
soul, which I have divined from her performance and her
work, the truth is, beyond "Could you sign my friend's
T-shirt?" I didn't have anything to say to her that would
have spanned the distance between what I wanted to say
and what was socially appropriate. What you are thinking is, *When I broke up with my last girlfriend I listened to your
second album over and over again until the grooves turned white,* *
and what you say is, "I've been a big fan of yours for a
long time." What you think is, *The very first time I went to
Festival I heard that song and somehow you and that song are
inextricably linked in that and every Festival experience I've had
since,* and you say, "I saw you at Festival!" You sit for two

---

*This is a historical reference for those of us born and func-
tional before 1982. In those dim, gray times before CDs we
had "records," or "albums," which were larger than CDs and
more fragile (they scratched easily), and if we played an
album too many times the needle would wear on the vinyl and
the track we were playing would literally turn whitish. If you
doubt this, I have a whole crate of used albums waiting for
their comeback in my basement and I can show you. To this
day it annoys me to pick up a CD I haven't played in a long
time and have to read all of the song titles and try to figure out
why I bought it—on an album, it was the gray track.

and a half hours and listen to this woman pour out her
most intimate secrets, and at the end you are ready to
say, "*Okay, I'm ready to begin a relationship with you, I think
we should be friends, let's go have coffee and I'll tell you a little
about me and we can make this sharing thing work*," and what
you say is, "I really liked your concert/readings/
work/songs/last CD."

I have been reflecting on what it must be like to be a
cultural icon. Hard, lonely work. They give themselves
away to strangers, and they stay strangers. They have all
of this emotional intimacy surrounding them, willing—
needing—to be shared . . . But they can't share it, except
perhaps in the most unusual situations, because it's an
illusion, a one-way mirror.

It occurs to me that that is the part of concerts and
public readings and performances of all variations that I
dislike, that moment when you realize, "Yes, but—*she*
doesn't know *me*." And the myth of intimacy is shattered,
and I go home.

I really enjoyed the concert.

I have most of your albums.

Your work has touched my heart.

Somehow it seems important that I let you know
that.

guitar lessons

i was in high school during the sixties when good music was invented.

There were radios and stereos and noisemaking instruments before the sixties, of course, but I had the excellent fortune to come along at exactly that moment when music changed from the stuff my parents liked to My Music. The harmonies and rhythms and lyrics and particularly the guitar riffs spoke directly to my soul. It was as if I woke up one day to a chorus of Bad Boys (so few even pretended to be angels) singing about the way I looked at life, the people I loved, the very core of who I was. My heart and soul was in this music. When I tipped my head back and crooned along with the radio, I sang with conviction and a solid sense of kinship.

The sixties, as we experienced them here in the Midwest: all appliances were avocado green, rust brown, or burnt orange. Shag carpeting was so cool that some people ran it right up their walls. Some fool discovered paisley. It was widely rumored—although never proved—that the lyrics to Jefferson Airplane's "White Rabbit" had something to do with drugs. Boys could get thrown out of school for having long hair. A boy's hair was "long" when it touched the collar of his shirt. The issue of being able to choose our own hair length was a serious one at my high school, one that was fought vehemently on both sides. We were rebels. Rugged individualists. Down with the Establishment.

Although my parents (bless their hearts) continued acquiring material goods just as fast as they could afford them, the overall feel of the era was flavored by the back-to-the-basics people who eschewed big agriculture, the chemical poisoning of the earth, rampant overconsumption of superfluous goods, and red meat. They lived on their own land and grew their own food, educated their own children, and purified all of our souls. My family never even met anyone like that, but their values still carried influence on the style of the times. Anything requiring rigid structure, too many machines, or too much technology was suspect. "Artificial" described things bad, "natural" described things desirable. As the civil rights movement gained credibility, "isms" were systematically identified and deemed bad: racism, ageism, classism, sexism. We would all be equal on the playing field. These were all new ideas in the sixties, raw and uncomfortable and slightly against the grain. We were re-inventing ourselves.

Because we were all equal and because we were all dedicated to giving our brothers and our sisters a hand up, any one of us could do anything we wanted to do. We had only to spread our wings and we would soar. We could be artists or CEOs. All any of us needed to be, for instance, Eric Clapton, were the tools, the inspiration, and parents who would be willing to tide us over until our bands took off.

In the mid-sixties I had not yet heard of Clapton, but I had shopped around for shortcuts to fame and fortune and I had made my choice. I decided to be a star. I wanted to be like Mason Williams and I saved my hard-earned cash to buy a guitar so I could teach myself to play "Classical Gas."

This ambition describes my musical acumen in so many ways. Skipping lightly over the notion of teaching yourself how to do something you don't know how to do, I did not really catch the fact that when Mason Williams himself played "Classical Gas," he did so with a guitar, an accompanying banjo, and a full orchestra behind him. I also skipped over one of the words in the title of the song that might have suggested a rather broader background in music theory and education than the one I brought to my guitar. If I had taken up the flute, it would have been to single-handedly play the *1812 Overture*.

There were a few other smaller problems with my budding career as a star. The instrument—particularly the secondhand $35 version of the instrument I had—can be hard to tune. Even more difficult if the ear doing the tuning can distinguish sharp from flat, but has no idea what—for instance—"C" might sound like.

There were other complaints I began to file almost immediately against the instrument:

- The strings hurt my fingers. When the pain stopped, my fingers were covered with calluses that interfered with my sense of touch.
- The instrument is so designed that the greatest dexterity is required from the hand my brain does not

favor. I can barely maneuver a pair of pliers with my left hand—why should I be able to finger chords with it?

- Playing the guitar requires an innate sense of rhythm. I have an innate sense of rhythm. It is not, shall we say, the workhorse of the organism. Much like my sense of pitch, my sense of rhythm is relative. When challenged by unexpected complications (wrapping left-hand fingers around the note F, for instance) my sense of rhythm adapts to the circumstances. This annoys my audience more than it does me.

I was not relying solely on the guitar to sweep me into the world of rock music—I also planned to sing. I was born for this career choice, I believed, because even as a small child I remember sitting on the back steps and singing my heart out. I wrote all of my own music, as a child. As I recall the process, I was unfamiliar with the mechanics of composing music so I simply sang an ever-changing panoply of notes on the theory that a song was in there somewhere and my job was to stumble into it. I remember being encouraged to spend a lot of my time outside, breathing "fresh air" and finding "something to do," which suggests that my musical writing style was hard on my mother's nerves.

In fact, my mother never did warm to my singing career. When I threw my fifteen-year-old heart and soul into "House of the Rising Sun," for instance, I might find my mother standing in the doorway, her face artificially solemn as she would muse, "I wonder what they do

there?" And then she would burst out laughing, destroying my entire creative ambiance. I took this to mean my
mother didn't believe I had the life experience to draw on
to properly render the lament of a prostitute. With other
songs—particularly those that required complex finger-
ing—I might glance up and find my mother lurching
through the room, fingers snapping, head bobbing, hips
swinging, as if she were having some unusually rhythmic
spastic fit. I could often gauge exactly how close I came
to hitting the high notes by her wince. I asked her once
if I had a good singing voice, and she said, "Well,
honey—it's *loud* . . ."

Another problem with my musical career was that
practicing the guitar ate viciously into my free time. I
needed time to wander the gravel pit and write cathartic
stories in my head. I had imaginary characters to nourish and develop. I did not have time to sit around sawing
the skin off the tips of my fingers and discovering for the
umpteenth time that my fingers still would not go from
here to there in the time the music allowed them. I spent
more time tuning the damned guitar than I did playing it,
it ate up my discretionary allowance in replacement
strings and sheet music, and no matter how much I practiced, the next time I took my guitar out of its case my
entire family scattered like cockroaches suddenly
exposed to light.

I found the field of music rigid and restrictive. A
child of dubious accomplishment and self-confidence, I
found refuge in English classes where language skills
came easily to me and where I discovered that the ability
to say something really well could sometimes obscure

even what I was saying. I loved music, and I thought fondly of music as a sister art. However, the actual manufacture and production of music owes an inordinate debt not to the whimsy of the muse, but rather my old nemesis, the Mistress of Math. This was an unwelcome discovery for me.

My sister the UnWee, who was for many years a professional musician, also played the guitar briefly. She was the one who tried to tune my guitar for me for a while, then held it up to her eye as if she were sighting a rifle and said, "The neck is warped." This is apparently a bad thing in a guitar, at least for many people. For me it was just one of the many ways I found, through the years, to bolster the careers of my fellow musicians. We may all still be equal, but there is one less player cluttering up the field.

Curiously, as a result of my efforts to teach myself the guitar I do still think of myself as, if not a musician, at least as a kindred spirit. An appreciator. I'm not a failure as a guitar player—I'm just not a very good one. Having tagged along behind for maybe half a block, I have a greater appreciation for the journey of those who are very good. And when so moved, I still throw my head back and sing along.

limping toward pro-earth

i admit it freely, easily, to anyone who asks: I am a recovering flash-and-trasher. If someone sold it, I bought it, used it, broke it, and threw it away. Flash the cash, bash and trash. There was not an earth-friendly bone in my body.

I remember twenty-five years ago nearly screwing myself into the floor with embarrassment when a luncheon companion took issue with the foam containers that came with every Big Mac. McDonald's, she informed the counter clerk, was single-handedly filling the planet with toxic, nonbiodegradable ozone-killers and any day now we would be sucked by the vacuum of outer space through the hole in the sky and scattered across oblivion. She wanted a foam-free hamburger. (Actually I think it was worse than that. I think she was a vegetarian and she wanted a meat-free, foam-free hamburger with no tree-killing paper products involved in its delivery. I remember looking up at their sign, which boasted

200,000,000 HAMBURGERS SOLD

and wondering why at least one of us was there.)

The counter clerk, who was about twelve and who had only just concluded his course on How to Handle Unreasonable Customers, blinked at her and he said, very seriously,

Well, if you don't want it, you can always throw it away.

This did not have the pacifying effect on her that he had anticipated.

She described overflowing landfills, hideous toxic substances leaching into the drinking water of innocent children, global warming, the disappearance of the rain forest, the systematic destruction of the Asian tiger, the African elephant, the Chinese panda, and a host of small songbirds right here in Michigan, all caused by the foam packaging foisted upon an innocent planet by McDonald's, Inc.

My friend was years ahead of her time, and too young and too dedicated to her cause to ask herself what having one twelve-year-old counter clerk take her hamburger out of a foam container and hand it to her — and then throw the used container away — would do to save the world. She was going to save it that day, right there, in that restaurant.

To calm her, he put it in a paper bag.

To be honest, she was not the most stable friend I had, and it occurred to me, as she went off on a tangent about deforestation and slash-and-burn economics, that she perhaps had less fear of being hauled off to jail for Excessive Political Integrity than I had.

It was a long time before I ventured into any McDonald's with a vegetarian again.

In fact, the sins I have committed against my planet were ghastly and almost unrelenting for a good twenty-five years.

And then I fell in love.

With a woman who devotes one day a week to shipping worms to people.

People who hardly ever go fishing. (This is, in fact, a touchy subject.)

Or perhaps these people do go fishing: I've seen these worms, and they are way too skinny to fit any hook I've ever used.

These worms eat people's garbage.

When I walked into her house, there were four separate trash bins on her back porch.

When I helped her wash dishes, she washed tin cans. Plastic milk cartons. She spoke some sort of secret code revealed to her by mysterious markings on the bottoms of plastic containers.

Oh my God, I thought, *This woman is a recycler.*

This will never last.

Worms do not eat my garbage. I don't cook. The worms would starve. I've been told they don't care at all for secondhand cat litter, so they are useless to me.

I have, however, begun recycling water cartons. I buy my water by the gallon, six gallons at a time, and the cartons began building up on me. I decided to recycle. I recycle by stomping on the plastic cartons and throwing them into a plastic bin.

There is something wrong with my method, however. I'm not sure what.

So far, they have not biodegraded. They have not

recycled. They haven't done much of anything that I can see. They just accumulate. The back porch is nearly full now, and I can see no changes taking place even to the very first cartons I put out there.

I am resisting the urge to throw them all into a big plastic bag and toss them in the trash.

jasmine

i am watching jasmine sleep.

I took the day off work for that express purpose. At eighteen she is my oldest cat (thirteen years Babycakes' senior), and she has made it clear she does not expect to stay with me forever. Her bones creak and her joints are stiff and, although she is fond of me in her own way, I can sense that she has been preparing for a transition.

She is at this moment curled up like a small black ball on the quilt on my waterbed, not unlike a small wad of roadkill. She hasn't moved since I got up this morning. I am in the computer room, where I can lean back and crane my head around the monitor to study her through the doorway. From time to time I watch her intently, or I get up and go peer over her until she breathes. It is and is not my fault she is in the condition she is in today, and I am struggling — belatedly — to be responsible.

Yesterday I was late for work because, in the final upheaval between responsibility, good pet ownership, and the sporadically hectic schedule that has become my life, I took a few hours off work to take her to the vet and have her put under so they could shave the mats that have been growing in her coat since last spring. At first I thought she would take them out, and then I thought they would grow out, and then I thought I would take them out. I was wrong three times in a row. At eighteen she has considerably more patience with me than she had when she was younger, but even that does not extend to spending hours in uncomfortable positions while a deranged human cuts off her coat with a pair of dull scissors. So knowing (and not really processing) the risks, I took her to the professionals and had her shaved.

When I came back later to pick her up they brought her to me in her carrier and I peeked in. She was lying on her back with her back legs pulled up like a stunned rabbit. The vet told me to leave her in the carrier for the next few hours and to not let her eat too much right away. I took her home. It became clear to me very short-ly that fully half of the cat was nonfunctional, and even hours later when I released her from the carrier, the back half of the cat stumbled and fell over sideways. I gave her a little food and left her downstairs, thinking she would stay. Sometime later I found her hanging from the end of the waterbed, too stuck by the front claws to get loose and too weak in the rear to heave up.

I immediately concluded she had had a stroke or had suffered some unknown spinal damage. I spent the night trying not to move (after knocking her over and nearly crushing her when I crawled in) and I mourned her, con-vinced that I would have to take her in this morning and have her put down. At two o'clock this morning she was still navigating in figure eights, compensating for erratic rear-end flops, rather than walking.

But when I woke up this morning, she was moving better—not as well as she should, but much better. I called the vet, who assured me it is probably just a matter of age. She is very old for a cat, and it takes her system a long time to fight off the anesthesia.

So she is sleeping, and I am watching her sleep. She is my oldest cat, and certainly the longest-lived of any I've had. She has made relatively few demands of me in her life. When I got her, as a gift from my brother, she sat in the palm of my hand with her back to me. I had never seen a kitten so tiny or quite so aloof, and for most of her life she has held both standards. In her prime she was beautiful, exquisitely groomed, with the short nose, the round eyes, and the classically sweet expression that is a black cat. As she has grown older, she has taken on a more ragged appearance, but she has become friendlier.

In fact, in our shared activities, I have found a standard that describes her size and her brand of affection perfectly. Curled up in a ball to sleep, she occupies exactly three-quarters of a mouse pad.

It seems a little odd to write without her.

penis envy

i never thought i was a tomboy. Tomboys conjured up images of little girls with bad haircuts, gender-inappropriate clothing, and some sort of snickering dirty joke I never quite got. Tomboys, I read from the subtext of the adults around me, were somehow imitations. Wannabes. (I have never met a tomboy to whose face I would say that yet— I'm merely reporting the mood of the times.) I skipped that whole throw-a-bowl-over-your-head haircut, spit, kick dirt, and use bad words stage of gender self-definition. Forget being a tomboy: I wanted to be a boy.

Boys could wear jeans. To school. Most of the boys I knew lived in jeans seven days a week. (Even better, I'll swear some spent all seven days in the same pair.) Boys popped out of the womb with that amazing, universally accepted motherthing that excused them from having manners or brains or consideration or even the need to curb their sexual instincts. *Oh, you know . . . he's a boy.* Somewhere during my school career it became social law that we all had to find little underskirts, fill them so full of starch that they crackled when we walked and stuck out almost horizontally from our waists, and then we had to catch them, somehow jump on top of them, and sit on them all day. Boys never did stupid shit like that.

In fifth grade we were broken up into groups — girls and boys and taken to secret hidden places in the schools where we girls were told our bodies would soon turn on us, start leaking disgusting bodily fluids without notice, and our hormones would throw us into hysterical rages and unaccountable weeping sessions. We couldn't wait to find out what would happen to the boys — they already leaked disgusting bodily fluids and we'd been advised of their congenitally poor impulse control even before this new twist came along. The boys came back to class looking smug and mysterious and every last one of them had a new comb. *So, tell us*, we would whisper during class. *What godawful thing is your body going to do to you soon?* They looked blank. *What was your meeting about?* we demanded. They said, *Grooming.*

Cramps, bloating, mood swings, walking down the hall in eighth grade to have a friend come up, cover you with her coat, and whisper, *You have blood all over the back of your dress* . . . versus shaving little hairs off your chin once a day. Give me a razor. (Imagine my aggravation a year or so later.)

I cried when my mother dragged me to a store to buy me a bra. In the first place the one we bought was too tight and it began gnawing into my shoulders and under my shoulder blades almost immediately — but it was a *bra*. It meant my body was determined to stay a girl in spite of the clear and ever-present evidence that a horrible mistake had been made.

Just about everything about boys fascinated me except the boys themselves. Boys were rude and crude and there was apparently no end to the jokes they could make about the same body part. They were mean to each other. They were mean to me. They could tease you until you cried and they would laugh and snicker and poke each other in the ribs and tease you some more, but God forbid a *boy* ever got hurt. He would freeze all of the muscles of his face until they quivered, one single tear would leak out of one eye, and the whole world came to a stop. National headlines screamed:

WOUNDED BOY BRAVE IN THE FACE OF PAIN

Coldwater, MI: Despite cruel and bitter teasing by local feral girls, Brave Boy Number One has refrained from tears. Upsucking like the trooper he is, Brave said, "I'm sure she's just having a bad day. I'm just glad I have the the stones to take it." Local authorities have planned a special recognition ceremony for Brave on Friday, July 12, at the American Legion in Coldwater. Blinking courageously, Brave remarks, "My uncle from California may fly in . . ."

I'm not bitter. When I was a kid these were the boys for whom the gyms were built and the sports equipment was purchased. They were the boys who copied my German homework (a dangerous practice in itself) so they could sleep off a too-late night before and still keep up their grade point average to be able to stay on the baseball team. They were the boys who proudly told me one of their buds had knocked up some girl, but they were all going to go down to the friend of the court and "admit" that each and every one of them had slept with her so the friend wouldn't be hung with paying child support the rest of his life. I don't know if their plan worked; I do know none of them could see anything wrong with it. They were just being boys.

My cousin got caught driving drunk when he was sixteen or seventeen and his father had to come bail him out of jail, a story my uncle told with that rueful, what-can-you-do-he's-a-boy grin. It was a wonderful family story. Had I done the same thing I would have been lucky to get out of jail and doubly lucky to have a home to come to.

I know a lot of wonderful men. Gentle, kind, enlightened men. A great many of the mannerless ruffians I grew up with managed to grow up to be decent, considerate men. Some of my closest friends are men, and I cherish their presence in my life.

About the only time I get angry now is when local, state, or national governments start to think about writing legislation about allowing gay marriages or living-together partners health coverage. You can count the seconds until up pops a man—just about my age—and he starts waving the American flag and babbling on about "special privileges" and "special rights" and the purpose of the flag, the Constitution, and the American Way of Life. Every time he does, I want to say, "I know you, and brother—you've had 'special privileges' and 'special rights' your whole damned life. Sit down, shut up, and let the rest of us have a chance."

the rose-colored ice

i used to skate like Dorothy Hamill. I used to swoop and glide around the ice with my little skating skirt swirling and my long, elegant tresses flying in the wind . . . It would have been hard for the casual observer to see my little skating skirt swirling under the insulated snow pants my mother made me wear, and my long, elegant tresses regularly fell victim to my mother's scissors, but a girl can dream. No girl ever dreamed of looking like the Pillsbury Doughboy on ice.

Realistically I suspect I could rate my skating talents right around Could Stand Up, but skates are wondrous things for the young. Racing across the ice, cutting abrupt turns, making that sharp, slicing-ice sound could make any child feel like a born athlete. I could feel every muscle in my body moving in perfect harmony with speed and grace and balance. I was quick and agile and when I fell I slid a good fifteen feet, as if that were in fact the very maneuver I had intended.

I remember spending a great deal of my childhood skating on the frozen ponds behind my house. Winters were longer when I was a child (particularly the frozen part), and more perfectly suited to winter sports. Hours, of course, were longer and not quite so evenly measured.

The cold was friendly, the wind was irrelevant, and when I was a child and had just spent hours doing exquisitely graceful pirouettes on the ice, chili and oyster crackers were a nearly perfect meal. (For the record, should anyone feel the need to feed me, I detest chili. I am fond of oyster crackers.) I don't remember why I quit skating. Bad winters, perhaps. I may have outgrown my skates. For reasons I can no longer remember there came a long period of time when I didn't skate at all.

In college I discovered that my roommates and I lived half a block from a public skating pond. I spent ten dollars on a pair of skates for my birthday (serendipitously in January) and I convinced my friends to go down to the pond with me. I had visions of awing them with my skills and grace. I tied on my skates, stood up, and realized almost immediately that Dorothy Hamill must have skated *every* day. I had failed to take several sensations into account when I spoke so eloquently to my gullible friends about the joys of skating. I had forgotten what it feels like to have ankles made of damp noodle material. I had forgotten that ice is cold. I had forgotten that ice is not only cold, it's hard. Ice is amazingly hard. Ice can take your breath away. And when it does, it gets even colder. Your gloves, your left ear, even the seat of your pants will begin to stick to it. My friends discovered in very short order that the best part of ice skating was leaving the ice, and a few warming beers didn't hurt.

I paid money not too long ago (well, someone paid money—I think the trip was a birthday present for me) to watch Dorothy Hamill skate. I must have misplaced

my skates the last time I moved, and I have a written list
of weak joints and potentially breakable bones right here
in my pocket just in case anyone offers to buy me a new
pair—and to be honest, I'm just not all that enamored
with the concept of ice anymore—but there was
Dorothy Hamill swirling around on the ice in her elegant
little skating skirt, making it all look like a child could do
it. And I am secure in the knowledge that when I was a
child, I could.

lines in the sand

not long ago a friend and I were talking (I was talking) and she reminded me that working for twenty-five years as a caseworker for the department of social services could easily color my opinions of people in general. I had to stop and think about that. She's right. It probably does. We had been talking about men, and in the work I do men come and go (some more violently than others) but women and children are the meat and potatoes of welfare. Even reformed welfare.

We are all potential victims of reactive, reflexive thinking. In my job, for instance, we butter our bread with emergencies. The first time someone called me to tell me the electric company was sitting in their front yard ready to disconnect their power, I thought, *Oh my God, I have to drop everything and solve this crisis for my client.* Ten years and several thousand power disconnections later I thought, *So . . . what happened to all of those steps between missing a payment and the arrival of that truck . . .* When I deal with people in crisis their crisis may last anywhere from a few hours to a few months. When all of the issues in their lives that I can assist them with are resolved I don't hear from them anymore. I don't notice they are gone because there are so many other families in crisis to take their place. Thus for something like twenty-five years my relationship with my clients has begun, "I need . . ." More often than not I don't have the tools to give them the help they want. I can patch, but I can't heal. And throughout this continual abrasion of too many problems versus too few solutions, there is a natural self-protective process that takes place not unlike a callus forming on the heart.

Today my friend Annie and I went to lunch and I was complaining about some serious obstacle in my life (a train, if I remember correctly, hurtling along directly between me and my lunch) and Annie answered, "Oh sure—someone's four-year-old child is hit and killed by a car, but in the overall scheme of the universe I'm SURE the fact that you had to wait on lunch for a train is the truly important issue."

I don't have a four-year-old child, dead or alive, but I'm fairly sure I would feel terrible if someone ran over her: my grief might even outweigh my aggravation with not being fed. I said, "Whose child is dead?"

She said, "The guard's."

We are protected from the more demonstrative of our customers at work by security guards, many of whom—before we wooed them out of poverty with the promise of minimum wage—were (or still are) our customers. I said, "What guard?"

Annie said, "The woman on the second (my) floor. The *only* woman, right now."

I pride myself on my powers of observation.

I persevered. "When did the kid die?"

"Last night."

This at least explained how the child had wedged herself between the Amtrak and my lunch. "What happened?"

What happened was the woman came in to work this morning to tell her boss her four-year-old daughter had been killed in a car accident the night before, and she had to get to Kentucky, where the child lived with her mother (the child's grandmother). She didn't have any money. Being a kind and caring man, he gave her bus fare and some spending money and put her on a bus to Kentucky. Then—instead of celebrating his fiftieth birthday, which was also today—he started taking up a collection from people in the building to help out this woman who had to go home to bury her daughter.

The grief-stricken mother called her boss from the bus station in Detroit to tell him she'd called her mother in Kentucky and learned that her child had died, but they had revived her; they had not told her (the mother) this because they did not expect the child to live. So she was very likely still going home to bury her child.

He felt terrible, because if he had known that, he would have given her airfare and flown her down, rather than have her rattle to Kentucky for the twelve-plus hours it must take to get there on a bus.

Nonetheless, the train passed and—properly chastened—I had an excellent lunch.

I don't know where she was when she called him again to tell him she had called the hospital and the child had "mumbled something" to her before the nurse took the phone and told her—the distraught, bus-riding mother— that the hospital would need $200 immediately to keep the child in the intensive care unit another day . . .

He experienced a moment of doubt. Perhaps he's been in a hospital at some time in his life. Perhaps he's actually seen a bill for one day of intensive care. But he assured her he would wire her the $200, and she could pick it up at the window of the bus terminal in Kentucky.

And then he called her mother, to ask how the little girl was doing. The grandmother answered, "She's fine — she's playing outside, right now . . ."

And then he called the police.

But he feels terrible. He's out whatever he gave her for the bus ticket, plus whatever he gave her for expenses for the trip. He feels like a fool because he told everyone in the building this heartwrenching story about a dying child who isn't dying. And he's embarrassed because he believed her. Felt sorry for her. Did more for one person in one day than I have ever done for anyone not immediately related to me in my lifetime. And it was a scam.

He did nothing he should feel badly about.

I would have been willing to assume that — whatever it was — she had *some* pressing need for a bus ticket to Kentucky. I was not raised that way, but then, I have never been desperate and without resources, either. Sometimes people just have to take what they need. In a perfect world sometime they'll be the taker, and another time they'll be the giver. Or, in a perfect world, there will be enough givers with enough to give to meet the needs of the needy.

And in the balance of life, I would rather get taken for doing something I thought was good than live with knowing I refused to help someone who needed me because I had lost the ability to care.

mine

as i was standing in the break room today one of my coworkers was rifling through our silverware drawer and she pulled out some sort of eating/cooking implement and said, in mild amazement, "That's mine." And she dug a little more and found something else that belonged to her, and yet one more thing, and, amazed at this unexpected booty, she said, "My daughter and I were just talking about this last night—all of our silverware is disappearing."

Being truly my mother's child, I said, "I can just hear this conversation—you blamed it all on your daughter, didn't you?" And I told her the saga of the rollers.

My mother—who, I presume, in the beginning may have been an actual sane woman—had three girls in five years, and all of us had hair. Furthermore, we grew up in an era when merely having hair was not sufficient: the goal for the women of the sixties was BIG HAIR. It had to stand up three inches above your head and stretch out three inches beyond each ear and it had to be LONG. Long and fat and, not curly, not corkscrewed, not tangled, but thick and uniform and just ever so slightly *bent*.

Whatever gene causes that kind of hair has never fallen anywhere near our family tree. I have a great many strands of hair on my head but each individual strand is very fine and all of them pulled together still don't amount to much. My hair curls on whim, but the only whim it has ever recognized is its own. I could roll it up and tease it and spray it and tease it and spray it until my arms fell off and I could step back, gaze critically into the mirror, and watch my handiwork split down the center into an apparently divinely decreed part, and fall. Flat. Lifeless. As unstyled as string, hugging desperately to my skull and frizzing without mercy on the ends.

My next younger sister, the UnWee, a strawberry blond, wrapped her hair every night around orange juice concentrate cans, and while she managed to have big, fat, uniform, slightly bent hair, she also had a disposition that would have frightened a grizzly bear. All through the big hair era she was a walking study in sleep deprivation.

Our youngest sister, the Wee One, had thick, dark, straight hair—beautiful hair. As a child she was often compared to an Indian baby. Her hair grows easily, and she grew it long. And rolled it on giant rollers. And watched the curl fall out faster than it fell out of mine.

My mother wore her hair short. It was brown, naturally, but the exact shade of brown changed with her mood, slightly less frequently than the hide of a chameleon. She cut it herself, she colored it, she styled it, she permed it, she rolled it and styled it again. My mother was so familiar with hair and its grooming needs that whenever she grabbed a brush and looked at us, we girls all ran for the back forty in rank terror. Our mother could yank out snarls like burrs from a horsetail, and those of us who had not had our skulls snatched senseless lived in terror of her deft hand. One of my earliest memories is of being smacked on the bare leg with a hairbrush for squirming too much while she ripped all of the hair off the nape of my neck.

So there were three aspiring, and one accomplished, women in a one-bathroom house. My father got up early in the morning, before any of us had stirred, and snuck out the back, preferring to stalk down and kill his breakfast in the relative anonymity of public restaurants to being anywhere near that bathroom when the women woke. Our little brothers slept in as if their shorter lives depended on it. That left the four of us to fight for hot water and jockey for mirror space.

We had two sets of tools to work with: a mismatched, half-broken, half-missing potpourri of stuff, and those crisp, efficient hairstyling weapons our mother labeled "MINE." She had a number of theories she used to support this decree. We lost everything, she said. None of us, she said, had ever in our lives actually ever put anything away where it belonged, and she could never FIND anything. She had to Go to Work. So she bought this one, and this one—by God—is MINE.

Guided by such a sharing spirit, we of course hoarded every hairstyling implement we could lay our hands on. Once while washing the family dishes I lost my head and tried to throw away what looked to me like a used orange juice can and the UnWee nearly severed my right arm. Nor could our mother herself be trusted: more than once while she was stalking about the house, ripping out drawers, wagging her hairbrush at my sisters and snarling about how "NO one in this family can EVER put anything AWAY," I snuck into her bedroom to find the missing rollers scattered all over her dresser.

When I was a child these incidents told me a great deal about my mother.

Being her oldest and certainly her most impressionable child, I moved away from home shortly after she recovered from a serious illness and reprimanded me for taking too many liberties with her authority, because, as she explained to me, "This is MY house . . ." I was offended for almost a week. I had moved home to help her recover, I had been doing my saintly best and that was all the thanks I got . . . Four days later, in the comfort of my own house I caught myself midstream in a lecture to my cat about stealing my hairbrush, and I realized that my mother had been extremely ill—she had almost died—and while I of course was destined to be a much more understanding woman than she, it was indeed her house and I was happy enough to have her back in it. It may have been the only sin I forgave her for while she was still alive.

Like my mother, I have only to have owned something once to own it always and forever, no matter how many times I lend it to someone, give it away, or sell it in a garage sale. I had it once, so out there somewhere is at least one that is MINE. This may account for the four identical rakes now leaning against the wall in my basement. I bought one. I remember buying it. You show me a rake—it looks like my rake—it's MINE.

moats

Those of us who have moats
don't always recommend them.
They take years to dig
and sometimes a lifetime
to fill in again.
It's hard to come up with
enough volunteers
to keep the alligators fed.
The castles they surround
are cold and drafty
and sometimes excruciatingly
empty.
I was too young
when I dug mine.
I was frightened.
I didn't know how much safety
would cost me.

this morning there was a black cat lying dead in the road.

My new neighbors moved in about two weeks ago. I have to say "about." The house has been standing empty for over a year, a silent taunt to my father's single inflexible rule of conduct: *turn off the lights*. The house changed Realtors twice, and whatever showings occurred must have been during the daytime while I was at work. I knew it had been shown when the configuration of ever-glowing lights changed. The kitchen light would beam for three weeks, utterly unattended by human life, and then one day the kitchen light would be off and the basement and bedroom lights would be on. For someone raised by the electricity police, this was not altogether unlike Chinese water torture. Still, I'm not sure how long they had lived there before I noticed them: I noticed their cat.

Sleek. Beautiful. There is nothing quite as elegant, nor as regal, as a black cat.

And nothing quite as tempting as a red squirrel.

The greatest concentrations of red squirrels live across the road, where the neighbor man feeds them every morning by hand. When I first noticed him he had an old hairy gold dog of some retriever variation and

every morning he and the dog would patrol their property, looking for whatever it is that retired men and old
dogs look for. But eventually I realized I had not seen the
dog for a while, and the man had begun a regular practice of courting squirrels.

This also is not a custom that would endear my
neighbor to my father. My father, for as long as I have
known him, has carried on a no-holds-barred, take-no-
prisoners war against his mortal enemies, red squirrels
and woodchucks. In that order. Red squirrels invade his
barn, where they chew on, defecate upon, or store walnuts among all of his prized possessions. They are
"messy." There is, in my father's eyes, no life form lower
than a red squirrel. Woodchucks burrow under the foun-
dations of his outbuildings, not a trait my father admires
in an animal, but as far as I know they have never
chewed on his collection of *Playboy* magazines. Out of
deference to the other animal life in the neighborhood
my father bought a live-trap that he sets out in the back
yard and waits for woodchucks and red squirrels to walk
into. When one does, he picks up the cage, carries it over
to an old barrel he keeps for exactly this purpose, dumps
the animal in the barrel, and shoots it with a .22.

The black cat appeared next door, picking his or her
way carefully through the grass, and I realized I had new
neighbors. The configuration of lights had changed
again. There were boxes on the front porch and children's toys in the back yard. In the front yard there was
a black cat, tail idly lashing, attention riveted on the red
squirrels across the road. I thought to myself, *This is a
tragedy in the making.*

The road my new neighbors and I live on is deceiving. When I moved there I thought it was a minor side street, a small paved two-lane with a 35 mph speed limit. And it is a two-lane and it does have a 35 mph speed limit. Rarely has one speed limit been so universally ignored. At night, in particular, cars fly down our road like bullets toward a homicide. And while it may be just a little two-lane, it is one of two two-lanes that connect a small community to the southeast to the city where we live, and it carries, therefore, a disproportionate amount of through traffic. Traffic in a hurry. Traffic leaving as quickly as it comes. Traffic not overly concerned with the health and well-being of a small black cat.

Last Sunday I spied my neighbor cat winding his/her way through the hedge across the street, and I lectured my Beloved on the dangers of the road I live on. I volunteered to go next door and tell my new neighbors that the street is deceiving and that if they want their cat to survive, they will learn to keep him/her inside. But I don't know the new neighbors, and it is my philosophy to avoid getting to be too friendly with people who live too close to me until I have at least a vague sense of what they are like. Also a trait learned from my father. And perhaps delivering a lecture about the proper care of one's pet is not the best way to become acquainted with one's neighbors.

Last Sunday my neighbor spied her cat winding his or her way through the hedge across the street, and she walked across the street, picked up her cat, carried it back to the front yard, set it down, petted it twice, and went into the house.

I presume this made her feel better.

The cat stood there in the grass, eyeing the hedge. The cat lashed its tail. The cat cried, twice, a cry I have come to associate with personal dissatisfaction. The cat spied something worth stalking in the grass, and the stalk, while unproductive, led the cat closer to the road, and then, as luck would have it, right on across the road . . . The whole round trip, from hedge base to front yard to hedge base again, took less than five minutes.

Five days later I found a black cat dead in the road.

There are any number of black cats who live around me. I cannot swear that it was my new neighbor's cat that I passed this morning. Someone's cat died. And I felt, as I always do, a stab of sadness. A life was lost. A family pet is gone.

Welcome to the neighborhood.

the hysterical alarm clock

my alarm clock, which is not terribly old, recently
retired. It had been expressing minor job dissatisfaction—it kept losing the radio station it had been using to
wake me up every morning—but I was relatively
unalarmed until the morning I woke up to no alarm at all.
The clock was just sitting there in absolute silence over
my head, mutely reporting the time, which just happened
to be the precise moment when I normally close my house
door and leave for work. Were it not for the large gold cat
stomping in my left ear, I might have slept until noon.

On my way home from work I went directly to an
appliance store and bought a new alarm clock, this one
with a built-in CD player. I liked its look. I liked its
shape and substance. I have become covetous of CD
players now that I drive the only vehicle still on the road
that doesn't have one. As I was checking out, the diligent
young clerk inquired, "Are you replacing one that has
broken, or is this just a new purchase?"

I said, "My old alarm is not alarmed anymore—in
fact, it shows no concern whatsoever these days."

The young man touched the spot between his eyes
with his middle finger. He said, "Because they break, you
know."

"You expect this particular one to break?"

The young man gazed at me vacantly for a minute. He said, "But if you buy our service warranty for $9.95 you can bring it back at any time in your lifetime and buy a brand-new one for $9."

"Wouldn't it be simpler to apply the $9.95 to the technology of this one and build one that will never break?"

The young man looked around the store as if searching for a sign—from anyone, I suppose—indicating what he had done to deserve me. "So I'm assuming you don't want the service warranty," he said, and rang up my clock.

I had not slept well the night before, which is why I overslept at all.

My Beloved is a morning person. Morning people wake up with lists forming behind their eyes of all of the wonderful things they might do on this brand-new sparkling day. They spring gleefully out of bed—often humming or engaging in some other obnoxious behavior—and they are cheerful and prone to spontaneous bouts of calisthenics. All morning people pick night people for their mates because all morning people are just basically mean. However, because she is a morning person, she frequently not only wakes up, but *gets up*, before her alarm goes off. I never get up a second before I have to. In fact, I often get up seven minutes after I should have. Where my Beloved keeps an alarm so she can have something she can feel superior to, I keep one because I need it.

But I had not slept well, and as a result I was tired. On the night I hired my new alarm I plugged it in, set it, poked all of the appropriate buttons, and went to sleep early.

My alarm went off.

I remember thinking, *It feels like I just fell asleep*, but I couldn't tell what time it was because — and I find this confusing — while the new alarm plays the radio, it does not display the time. Apparently this is to thwart those of us who aim one eye at the digital readout and promptly punch the sleep button.

It seemed quite dark out. It was late fall and morning had been coming increasingly later . . . but this *looked*, to the untrained eye, like the dead of night.

So I sat up, fumbled for the light, and stared blearily at my watch, which said 12:00.

I had set the alarm for 6:30. It is not all that uncommon for an alarm I have set to go off at 6:30 in the evening, but I have never had one set for 6:30 go off at midnight.

So I turned it off.

Or, I pushed the button that said, "Off."

The radio continued, unabated.

I pushed the power button to "Off."

The radio continued singing.

I pushed the sleep button.

Sing, sing sing . . .

I dug out my glasses, fumbled around with the clock instructions, and read, *There are three ways to turn off the alarm*, and it listed them. I tried all three, first one at a time, and then in various combinations of two out of three, and then I considered throwing the machine through the window.

I turned the volume on the radio so low it no longer made noise: which achieved my immediate aim, which was to go back to sleep. I did not reset the alarm for a more appropriate time. Certain ironies seem very clear at midnight when you wish you were asleep and instead you are battling a hostile alarm clock, and one of them is that not only is it alarmed when you wish to hell it wasn't . . . the clock won't tell you the time.

And then, magically, it all corrected itself. The time returned . . . I gingerly restored the volume and the radio had gone to sleep . . . I should have considered this in more depth, but by this time my sole concern was sleep.

Which is where I went.

The alarm/radio went off.

I bolted upright, scowled suspiciously at the dark sky beyond my window, turned on the light, found my glasses, applied my glasses to my face and my watch to my glasses, where I ascertained it was exactly 12:22.

I poked every button, bar, and color change on that machine. I dug around in my desk for a pen and jabbed it repeatedly into a small hole labeled "reset." Finally I turned the volume off, and the machine became quiet again.

It refused to tell me the time.

In fact it sat there on my headboard slightly above and behind my head with just one red eye beaming the word "POWER" over my inert body.

I stabbed its single red eye repeatedly with my thumbs. No effect.

"Wake me up at seven tomorrow morning," I snarled at the cat.

There is always the possibility of operator error and I know this. Even with operator error, most power buttons I've pushed in my lifetime have either removed or restored the power—this one does nothing. The instructions are written in English words applied to Japanese syntax, but I believe the intended meaning is that the button will provide or remove power. I believe this machine does not work properly. I believe this machine is power-crazed. Possessed. I need to just yank the plug, deprive it of all power at the source, put it back in its box, and return it to the nice young clerk who wanted me to have a lifetime supply of timeless, hysterical alarm clocks.

I'm looking forward to this conversation.

I've been practicing.

professionalism

Yes
I understand that
but what am I to do
with my anger?
I am running out
of Mason jars
my supply of lovers
has grown thin
my friends all stare at me
with fixed and wary smiles
and yesterday my dog
ran off.

my valentine: the beginning

for years valentine's day has smelled faintly of crayons and white paste for me. A kid's holiday. It's been a long time since I've paid much attention to it. My romantic life, while rich and colorful, has also been largely imaginary. I have specialized in lusts-from-afar, those tremendously tumultuous, passionate, exhilarating, risk-free relationships a true dreamer like myself can have with people who have no idea they're in a relationship at all. Or perhaps they are entirely aware of their relationship—it just happens not to be with me.

Probably the last time I paid much attention to Valentine's Day I was sitting at my mother's kitchen table, painstakingly lettering out a cheap, gaudy card for every student in my class, taking exceptional care not to accidentally send any mushy or goopy one to a *boy*. (I had, apparently, even then an inkling of what was to come.) Boys were horrible things and I probably would not have wasted my good valentines on any of them, had it not been for a school rule that if you sent one valentine to anyone, you had to have a valentine for every member of your class.

I may have been somewhat oblivious to the spirit of the holiday. Each year we would beg a good-sized shoebox from our parents and lug it to school, where we would spend several art classes covering it with colored construction paper, cut-up paper lace doilies, and sprigs of tin foil and chewing gum (someone always ate the paste) for the Most Beautiful Box competition. I was a competitive child. I was an extremely competitive child. I needed to have the most beautiful box, and I needed to collect the most valentines inside my box. I also needed to eat the most pink-frosted cookies, have the most punch, and generally suck up attention like an alligator on a log soaks up sun. Attention—positive if possible, but in a pinch negative would do—was the fuel that made my motor run, and ruthless, endless competition was the way to achieve it. (It was about this time in my life that my mother encouraged me to read *The Bad Seed*.)

So it did not occur to me to give valentines to my friends because I liked them, any more than it would occur to me that people would give me valentines because they liked me. I expected valentines because I had the prettiest valentine box. I expected valentines because I needed to have more valentines than anyone else.

Surprisingly enough, I was not exceptionally popular in grade school. If you were to hunt up some of my fellow classmates, you might be surprised to discover I have not always been known for my sense of humor. You might find the little boy in fourth grade, for instance, who remembers mostly being kicked rather soundly in the shins.

⸺

I flirted with her the first time I met her because I never really thought it would come to much. I was just in that kind of mood that day.

I was flirting with her the second time I saw her when I told her that the thing I missed most about male/female relationships was the fact that women never flirt with each other. She actually let me get away with that.

And all of those interim times when we saw each other and exchanged our life histories and delved into each other's minds I kept telling myself nothing would come of it. Someone else would catch her interest. Sometimes when I felt nervous I would take out my old "if you *really* knew me you wouldn't like me" security blanket and suck my mental thumb.

Last year at Valentine's Day we were still feeling our way along that "I think I like her—very much—but it could all blow away next week . . ." dust-in-the-wind how-long-can-I-hide-all-my-faults stage of the relationship. She gave me a book and a beautiful card. I may not have given her anything.

Last week I was muttering under my breath about how ill-suited I am for a long-term, long-distance relationship, and there is every chance that I will eventually find myself muttering about that again.

But today I am thinking, "What shall I do for Valentine's Day?" I need glue. Red paper. Some pretty lace. Perhaps I can use my Dremel or some other rotary tool. A flower or two might be nice.

To my Valentine: I love you.

Wanna help me decorate my box?

babycakes is not a happy cat. He is pacing the house, voicing his discontent (for there is no reason to *have* discontent, he believes quite firmly, if it cannot be voiced) in each room, where he can monitor the acoustics for precisely the pitch of heartrending melancholy that will render unto Babycakes that which is Babycakes'.

There are packages full of Mommy's things by the door.

This can never be good.

In the first place, nowhere in any of these packages (and Mommy is known for her many packages) is his fine gold self. Not that Babycakes has any desire to go away with Mommy—he has had quite enough of those adventures, thank you very much. Each time Mommy has put him in a package and taken him away with her, he has wound up on a big, shiny, slippery serving tray on the pointed end of Jennifer Needles. Babycakes plans never to leave home again.

No, the crux of this problem is to convince Mommy she need never go away either. She could stay at home all of the time and be with Babycakes. She would have more time to stir his food whenever it grows stale. She would be in attendance to snatch away bad box smells and refresh them with new litter. They could sit together in the evenings and watch the flickerbox, and then in the morning they could sit together and watch the flickerbox again. Grooming a soiled ear, he rethinks this solution, examining it for unmet needs, but he can find none. The solution is perfect. Now for a plan.

He is a cat who thinks best on his feet. Pacing from room to room, he meows plaintively, cocking an ear for Mommy's obedient reply.

"Now what?"

Satisfied he has her attention, he paces to a farther room and calls again. This is a pleasant game and it passes the time nicely, but Mommy ruins it by appearing in exactly the same room he is in, seizing his fine gold self in her arms, pinching his fine white whiskers (and the one black one) in her hand as she gazes intently into his eyes and demands, "What do you *want*?"

Babycakes is so unnerved by this attack that he is stricken with the dreaded bonemelt. All of his supporting muscles collapse and all parts of his body not specifically held captive by Mommy dribble down toward the floor.

"Fine," Mommy snaps. "You are a bad bad bad bad *bad* cat," and sets him on the floor. This is the highest praise she ever gives him, and it means, "I'm sorry, you're right, I'm wrong, and I will never touch you without your permission again." She is sweet, but she can be a little slow.

Babycakes walks into the next room, looks around, considers his options, and cries. He is in Mommy's litter room now where the acoustics are particularly effective and carry the tone of his personal dissatisfaction all through the house. He reaches down and carefully grooms a few displaced hairs. She will come soon — if not to this cry, then the next. He flexes his toenails, eyeing them critically. If she ignores him again, he will choose something she had appeared to be fond of lately and he will dig it.

None of this will prevent her from leaving, of course: late in the evening, when she is miles away from him and trying to enjoy the company of whatever unimaginable force that has taken her away, she will frown slightly to herself and murmur, "I wonder if he's sick . . ."

One works with the tools one has.

everything i know about cars

everything i know about cars I learned from my dad. In my late teens and early twenties my dad went from being that surly stranger out in the garage to being one of the most important people in my life. He had to be: he was the only mechanic I knew who would work for free.

I got my first car when I was eighteen. I didn't have to go far to get it—it was parked out in the driveway. It was a 1960 Ford Galaxie station wagon, powder blue. It had been my mother's car but it had frozen in second and third gears simultaneously—something she insisted happened and my father maintained was physically impossible—and for the sake of their marriage they gave the car to me and bought her another one. At eighteen the last vehicle I wanted to be seen driving around town was a seven-year-old powder blue station wagon, but it was still worlds better than not being seen driving around town at all. The Ford was an instant lesson in the virtues and pitfalls of car ownership. It cost me, on average, $14 a week in repairs. Gasoline was 35 cents a gallon, but brake pads and fuel lines were nowhere near as forgiving on my budget. Like most older cars it had quirks. The flooring in the rear passenger side seat had rusted out so when I took friends with me I had to remember to warn them before they put their feet completely through my floor mat. It was an unpleasant drop that had a tendency to make them surly. The station wagon could be a little tricky about starting, and as time went by, the heater became less and less dependable.

My father and I did not communicate particularly well. Most of our conversations started with, "Hey Dad—you know that noise my car's started making . . ." This would be followed by a complex discussion of part names and practical functions and a lot of hand gestures where things sat over other things and even more things went through or over or around them, and eventually we would settle down to a discussion of price. The last conversation we had of this nature about the station wagon had to do with cams and rods and the joy of having a constant supply of oil in your crankcase. The wagon, for some reason, had run out of oil and now all of the cams had slid around in the wrong place and were unusually difficult to get back where they belonged. In fact, in the end, it never happened.

My father and I discussed oil and its amazing cooling properties any number of times over the next few years, but it took me a while to get the point.

It did not occur to me that changing the oil was a maintenance task on a vehicle. I'd never been responsible for a motor before; perhaps I just assumed they came with whatever oil they needed. My father changed the oil on the family car quite regularly—usually just minutes before we left on a trip—but my mother seemed to think this was excessive and badly timed and I assumed it was just part of their complex conversations about whether or not our father was going with us whenever we left the yard.

Are you going with us or not? Because I really don't care whether you go or you stay home, I just need to know if you're going . . .

(The sound of another oil can popping open.)

Once it became clear that the station wagon was going to spend the rest of eternity up on blocks in the back yard because my father *couldn't* fix it, I was forced to buy a new car. I paid $175 for a 1957 Chevy. Yes: I once drove a '57 Chevy. The cool '57 Chevy was, I believe, an Impala and mine was a Bel Air, but the models were almost identical. Mine was blue and white. It was twelve years old, but it was cool. It had a metal dashboard, and it came with a plastic coin holder that stayed on the dashboard by virtue of a magnet. It had no radio. The windshield wipers were not entirely reliable and the windshield had a tendency to steam up, but if I cranked the front vents open they would blow air on the windshield and hold back the steam. I loved my '57 Chevy.

Parts for the Chevy were a little hard to come by and it needed its fair share of them, but I had become accustomed by now to spending Sunday afternoons out in the garage with my dad, bored out of my mind and half-frozen, but diligently keeping him company while he fixed whatever was wrong.

From time to time I would mention to my dad the fact that the car shook. Vibrated. The body rattled so badly that I could no longer keep any change in the plastic magnetic change holder because it would bounce out. He would listen to me and then start drawing interlocking circles and pictures of parts and pieces fitting together again.

"Do you think it's serious?" I would check.

He would shrug. "I donno," he'd say.

My mother called square dances for years. It was a good job for her. It paid her a small income, it put her center stage among her friends where she enjoyed being, it catered to her love of music and dance. My father loves music, in his own way. Almost all of the musical artists he likes look something like Lorrie Morgan or Shania Twain. He is tone-deaf, rhythm is a foreign language for him, and he is happiest in the back of the room, possibly even with a pail over his head. Furthermore, there is not all that much for the husband of the caller to do at a square dance. He can either come up and help her demonstrate dances (see attention, rhythm, pail over head) or he can sit on the sidelines and watch everyone else dance.

My mother would warn him days in advance that a dance was coming up, and as the actual time to get cleaned up, put on a square dance outfit, and get into the car drew near, visions of our father would become vaguer and vaguer in our memories. Sometimes he would show up at the very last minute. Sometimes she would send us out to the back barns to fetch him. Sometimes he just . . . wasn't . . . anywhere. Sometimes they had huge fights over this, and sometimes she just spun gravel down the driveway and drove off without him.

We all learned to keep a low profile. Our house could be remarkably quiet around square dance time, given the fact that two adults and five children lived there.

One such storm had blown over and we children had all relaxed, assuming the adults had worked it out at least for that night, when my father appeared not far from me and murmured something about needing a ride. Could I take him out to where Mom was with her square dance club?

I had no idea where that was, but fortunately he did, and I loaded him up and drove him there. He sat scrunched down in the seat (it took him a full ten years to convince himself that something he had sired was actually capable of driving a vehicle) and said hardly a word to me for twelve miles. I parked in the parking lot, waiting for him to get out.

He said, "How long has it been doing this?"

I said, "Doing what?"

He said, "It shakes."

I said, "Oh, I told you about that—I used to keep quarters in the change tray on the dashboard. Now I can't keep the change tray on the dashboard and the quarters hop all over the car."

He pursed his lips. He nodded. He said, "You might think about selling it."

"You think it's serious, then," I surmised.

And—being my dad—he said, "I donno."

A few days after that my mother said to me, "Your father says you're selling your car . . ."

So I put my beloved '57 Chevy up for sale. I sold it for fifty dollars to a kid just out of high school. He was thrilled to get it. A week later the engine caught fire in the parking lot where he worked and the resulting damage totaled the car.

In 1969 or so I bought a 1964 Ford Fairlane. Fairlanes were economy cars for Ford, but they varied significantly in size and style from one year to the next. Some Fairlanes were land sharks: the '64 was about a four-person car, small, all-metal. When I bought it the back springs had gone bad and whoever owned it had welded his own makeshift suspension on the back, which consisted of two metal posts that semi-supported the springs. Whenever I drove the car over a slight rise, like backing out of a driveway, for instance, the back posts dragged.

I liked the Fairlane, but it taught me almost everything I know about car disorders. The fuel pump went bad. On the way through the back roads to visit a friend (I never seemed to go anywhere during normal daylight hours), for a while I was driving 60 mph and then I was driving 40 with the gas pedal floored, and by the time I got to her house I was driving 10.

The second or third time I ever drove it I decided to wind it out and see exactly what it would do. I topped out at 85 miles an hour. And then I flipped on my blinkers and decided to take the exit, stepped on the brakes, and . . . I had no brakes. Apparently I should not have been so nonchalant about the slight mushyness the brakes had had the last time I stepped on them. I drove that car down the exit, out onto the next road, almost a mile down that road, into a roadside park, and within six feet of coming back out on the road again before it finally coasted to a stop. So I learned to respect brake lines.

I also learned about chokes because the automatic choke on this car wasn't automatic. It stalled on hills (it was a standard transmission) it stalled at lights, it stalled almost anytime I changed driving speeds. For a while I had my roommates all trained to jump out of the car and push it off to the side of the road whenever I gave the word. For an assignment in a speech class (*describe how something works to group*) I borrowed an old carburetor from my dad and demonstrated the butterfly valve and what it did, explaining to my class essentially what I did in every intersection in Battle Creek for months.

When I was in high school almost anyone could buy a book on automobile repair—you could buy a book for your specific make and model—and take the car apart and put it back together again in their own garage. I have no aptitude with tools and no interest in getting my hands dirty or my knuckles scraped up, both of which my dad did on a regular basis, but cars back then were the sum of their parts. There was no mass of cables and hoses and rebreathers for emission controls. There were no computers. In fact when I was in high school the only computers any of us ever saw were in science-fiction movies and they took up entire rooms of buildings to do less than your average desktop will do now.

As I grow older there are some transitions I make without even thinking about it very much, and some transitions I will apparently never make. Most of today's cars all look alike to me. They are small and boxy and while they may have keyless remote entries and CD players and lights that come on automatically—a host of bells and whistles that the cars of my high school days never dreamed of—they are not *cars*. Cars were a lifestyle. Cars were who you were and what you could afford and how much of what you could afford you were willing to put into your ride. A Camry will get you where you want to go, but it's hard to feel that emotional bond with a little beige four-banger.

Sometime during the mid-seventies my Baby Brother bought himself a 1964 GTO—we called them "goats." This (1964) was the same year Ford came out with the first Mustang. The Mustang was a little car; the GTO was a midsized car. They were big, metal cars with metal dashboards and vinyl bench seats (buckets may have been an option—my brother's car didn't have bucket seats) and the four of us—our Baby Brother, the Wee One, the UnWee, and I—all went out to a bar to listen to a local band. On the way home we hit a deer. The deer flew up over the corner of the hood and disappeared, the GTO spun around twice on the highway, and we all walked away without a scratch. (The deer limped away.) I think about that adventure every now and then, not because it was all that spectacular, but because (a) there was not a mark on that car where the deer hit, (b) there were no seat belts in the car, (c) there would have been enough room in that car to comfortably seat two more people, and none of the people in my family are petite, and (d) by today's standards that car was huge and weighed probably half again what a current-model car that size would weigh.

When I was in high school cars were built to withstand damage in a crash. Cars today are built to take the damage and allow the people inside them to withstand the crash. They are smaller, lighter, and considerably more collapsible. Fifty percent of the bulk of a modern engine is devoted to emission controls to protect the environment. When something goes wrong with a modern car, the owner has to take it to a garage and hook it up to a giant diagnostic computer, not unlike one of the Borg.

I need to buy a new car soon—or at least a newer one. My stalwart truck, Hoppy, began throwing off parts in his tenth year faster than I could afford to put them back on and I gave him away to an eager young owner who could, if he had to, walk much farther than I can. For the time being I am driving the Landshark, a 1992 Chevy Caprice, which runs (sucking gasoline like a goldfish), but winter is coming on and who knows what another year may bring?

So I've been thinking about cars a great deal here lately. What car I bought. When I bought it. How old it was when I bought it, how long it ran, how much it cost me to run it. Buying a new car is like looking for a new partner, including that long search-and-court period . . . Personally, I'm still in mourning for the old one.

153,000 miles

First the wipers became manic,
giving up all lesser speeds
to fling themselves in cleansing frenzies
across the glass: then they redefined
"intermittent," stopping mid-wipe
for minutes, sometimes miles,
to burst back into sudden action
back and forth, back and forth,
until the right wiper finally died,
lying at the bottom of the glass, heaving
like a dying swan
while its companion still grimly
rocked the cab back and forth,
back and forth.

where the heart is

i went to a country school from kindergarten through second grade. Bidwell School. It was an old-fashioned schoolhouse, brick, where twenty-five students and one teacher labored over grades K–6. When I was entering third grade they closed my school and integrated us into town school, but until then I was bused every morning to a school less than half a mile from my house.

One day the bus driver would not let me off the bus. He called the teacher to come look at me, they conferred, everyone else piled off the bus into class, and the bus driver drove me home.

I was crushed. I loved school. I went to school every day. I cried, I promised to be good. I assured my teacher I hadn't done anything wrong, that my mother would NEVER understand if I came home. This appeared to have greatly amused the bus driver, who assured me I really hadn't done anything wrong and—he was relatively sure—my mother would understand. It is possible, I suppose, that I gave the impression my mother was an intolerant ogre who used school to get rid of me, but that was not the true issue: I was, then as now, a true Capricorn. I believed there was one specific place I was supposed to be and a time I was supposed to be there and at that time I was supposed to be in school.

My perfect attendance record was destroyed by pinkeye.

I was not allowed to go to school, I was thrust unceremoniously into the frightening and unsettling status of Displaced in the Universe, all because the whites of my eyes had turned pink. I had done nothing to turn them pink — until someone pointed it out, I was not even *aware* they were pink — and in truth, I could not understand the significance of a minor color variation in my eye whites . . . All of that innocence concentrated in one child and still I was sent home.

My mother took me immediately to the doctor, who prescribed sunglasses and a dark room and perhaps some pills or eyedrops or something, I don't remember. My mother bought me a pair of red sunglasses with miniature removable pistols in the holsters in the upper outside corners of each lens, and she tucked me into her bed, drew all the shades, and went off to do whatever it is that mothers do. The sunglasses were extremely cool and kept me entertained for ten or fifteen minutes — there is a limit to the available amusement to be gained from wearing sunglasses — and eventually I lost both pistols in the bedcovers, which pretty much jaded me to that whole experience. I found myself in the middle of my parents' bed in a semi-dark room. My eyes itched. Neither of my parents were there. I was alone. In the semi-dark. With itchy eyes, missing pistols, and the serious suspicion that being sick was not going to be any fun at all.

I do not remember my mother as being particularly solicitous of sick children, but that may have been because at that time she would have had three children at home, one age seven with itchy eyes and a distinct case of situational dissatisfaction, one three and a half with a passion for shredding anything she could get her hands on into tiny, tiny pieces she then stuffed into strange places, and a two-year-old who could toddle into any situation, given a minute, and whose sole communication tool was the word "No." I remember, as a child, being encouraged to get well again as soon as humanly possible. School was a wonderful place, I was told, and I should strive to be there every second possible. My mother, she told me, had always loved school.

Sometimes when I was ill—although I do not remember, just offhand, if she used this as a cure for pinkeye—my mother would make me a wonderful thing she called bubblemilk. Bubblemilk was almost worth getting sick for. I suspect it is illegal, if not immoral, to give children bubblemilk now: she poured milk, raw eggs, and sugar into a mixing bowl and turned it all into a rich, sweet foam. The other reward for being ill—although one nearly almost always had to throw up to get it—was lemon-lime pop. We never had pop at our house. It was too expensive and silly and wasteful until we began heaving like a herd of grass-eating puppies, and then out came the pop.

The other cure for childhood illness were the stock reports on WOWO. Any mention of hog futures always reminds me of being a small child, home, miserable and covered with itchy red spots, and listening to the Fort

Wayne radio station talk about hogs being up a quarter and beef down a half, and something about corn . . .

Pinkeye took me utterly by surprise, but as I grew slightly older I began to become aware of certain malfunctions in my anatomy. Sore throats. Inflamed tonsils. That general, overall, I-don't-want-to-be-here feeling. I reported all of these to my mother dutifully after an incident when I was detected by some teacher radar as being unfit to be taught and sent to the town school office, where my mother was called and ordered to come get me. I was entertained all the way home with a long, not entirely sympathetic discussion about exactly why I had failed to just say, "Mom, I'm sick, I can't go to school today." *Before* I rode the bus, infected everyone who would talk to me for several hours, and then inconvenienced my mother by making her come get me. I don't remember ever wanting my mother to come get me.

It would appear, from the available memories—all of which are solely mine—that I was rarely satisfied with the way I felt in the morning. That, or it is difficult to determine just how sick a sick child really is. By junior high I had determined that it was much easier to go to school than it was to endure her inquisition about *exactly* how sick I was. I interpreted this to mean she never believed me; that she believed, for some unknown reason, that I would *make up* an illness to stay home with her.

All of this reminds me of a story my grandmother used to tell me. She was the oldest child, her only brother nine years her junior. When he was five or six he began telling his mother that his heart hurt. His mother and his sister were of course immediately alarmed. Exactly *how* did it hurt? Under what circumstances did his heart hurt? He was a child and his answers were vague and confusing. Finally my great-grandmother said, "Show me *exactly* where your heart hurts." And he looked at her as if she had lost her one remaining marble, and he grabbed his knee and said, "Right *there* — in my *heart*." As a child who was served olives whenever I ordered pickles for several years, I understand how small mistakes like that are made.

So it may not have been disbelief on my mother's part that drove me to wobble, weak and riddled with germs, to school in order to escape her inquisition. I know, as an adult, *where* my heart is: this still does not always tell me whether or not I am too sick to go to work.

silly rabbit . . .

when i was a kid I believed it would have taken only one thing to make my life perfect—a horse. I wanted a horse so badly I could smell it. When I wandered off to the gravel pit, I always rode an imaginary horse. I collected china statues of horses. My favorite movie was *Tonka*, my favorite book was *The Black Stallion*, my favorite TV show was *Fury*. In fourth grade, my best friend got a horse. Every Christmas I closed my eyes (often months in advance—good preparation is important) and promised I would be completely satisfied if the only present I ever got—perhaps for the rest of my life—was a horse.

When I was a kid we lived on seven-eighths of an acre, which held our house, my father's garage, and the rambling, extended "shed" where my father kept his tools, his projects, and often himself. The rest was grass, which was a sacred crop for my father. My best friend's horse stepped on my father's lawn once, and I found my father out there, glaring at the horseshoe-shaped dents in his lawn hours later. He appeared to be in mourning. Eventually he became a professional groundskeeper, but when I was a kid he drove a delivery truck for a fuel oil company and later for a grocery company. My mother stayed home and made our home until I started high school. We had nowhere to keep a horse, my parents told me. We could not afford a horse. I took this to mean my parents did not want me to be happy.

My parents had a long history of keeping me from happiness, particularly when it came to animals. That I was even born aggravated their dog, Tinker, who grew to hate me. As soon as I was old enough, he led me out to the goat pen where my father's goat, Susie, would knock me down, stand on my suspenders, and breathe goat-breath in my face. The cat allowed us conditional permission to live in her home, but she lost no time establishing her boundaries where children were concerned. I developed a lifetime habit of good cat manners about four seconds after my first firm grasp of fur. I should have been suspicious, therefore, when my father brought home a rabbit.

I knew very little about rabbits. Wild ones lived in the yard. They did not appear to require any care. They were cute and furry and never made any noise, and their noses twitched.

Our rabbit was black and white. She was an adult when we got her. We named her Millie. I really don't remember how old I was when Millie came to live with us, nor do I remember ever asking for a rabbit, but for some reason her care was assigned to me. It was my job to feed her, water her, and keep her cage clean.

My first unpleasant discovery about Millie was that my father seemed to think I needed to feed her and water her *every day*. This cut into my personal social life something fierce. I complained from time to time, but he always pointed out that caring for a rabbit was nothing compared to caring for a horse. I had been wanting a horse for years by then and I was deeply suspicious no horse was going to be forthcoming, so I could hardly see why the comparative responsibilities even mattered, but he was on my case about that rabbit daily.

My next unpleasant discovery about Millie was that rabbits have been given uncommonly kind and misleading press. My father taught me to pick her up by gripping the nape of her neck and letting her feet dangle. He did not tell me this is because rabbits have a kick just slightly inferior to that of a kangaroo. I picked up my ten-pound rabbit, expecting a fuzzy, cuddly house pet, and she bared her toenails and tried to dice me. Then she started screaming. I was in no way prepared for the ungodly noises that an irate rabbit can make. Astounded, I looked into her pink eyes and determined she was possessed. Some perverse and malignant soul had transformed Flopsy into Hellspawn.

When I gave her fresh water she immediately crawled into the dish and spilled it, getting her bedding, herself, and, if she could, all of her food wet. She produced more rabbit pellets than she ate. She would sit out there in her cage behind the garage and make up lies to tell my father about how often she had been fed or watered. Every time that rabbit came up in conversation I knew automatically that words like "responsibility" were not far behind. I had determined that "responsibility" was a bad thing at a very early age, and personally did everything I could to avoid it. It had not occurred to me, before the rabbit came, that parents could just assign a responsibility to you, whether you wanted it or not, and then hold you accountable.

I never liked that rabbit. I hated every minute that I spent on her care. She made it clear there were no warm feelings she had to waste on me, either. Contrary to adult fiction, it is not a character-building experience for a child to realize she is actively hated by a bunny rabbit. All kinds of unresolved ego problems arise from situations like that. I could have been psychologically scarred.

I was a very rule-oriented child. Another child would have just set the rabbit on the ground and let the problem hop away. *I have no idea what happened to that rabbit, Dad—I turned my back on her for one second and the next thing I knew . . .*

I don't actually remember what happened to Millie. Perhaps my father grew tired of harassing me and found her a new home. Perhaps she died out of spite. I gave up rabbit tending without a single regret and went back to my pre-Millie life.

My father the groundskeeper, however, kept tending his grounds. A wide variety of wildlife grew in my father's grass. Salamanders were rare, but he grew three or four species of snakes, hundreds of frogs, a few stubborn moles, a turtle every now and then, and a fair number of wild rabbits. It was not all that uncommon, when I was a child, to look up and see my father racing across the lawn with his pitchfork poised overhead like a spear as he chased the offending mole or snake. It is perhaps images like that that make me the person I am today. My father's grass was never more than an inch tall, so most of his wildlife must have wandered in from the untended gravel pits and woodlots around our yard. When we still had the apple tree in the side yard, my father used to hunt the muskrats that came up in the fall to forage on the apples that had fallen to the ground. He chased them with a ball bat.

He had been mowing the day he came into the house carrying a baby rabbit in his hand to show us. The baby was barely an inch long, with too-short ears and a twitching nose. When I held it, I could feel its little heart beating in my hand. I knew immediately that I had to save it.

I had no idea what baby rabbits eat. Or, I assumed they drank their mother's milk, but I had no idea what rabbit milk was like. I picked grass for the baby and I put him in a refrigerator box in my father's shed, and every four hours I fed him evaporated milk through an eyedropper. We bonded immediately: he would not eat for anyone but me.

Unfortunately I had been invited to a slumber party that weekend. I suffered horribly over the moral dilemma the baby rabbit posed in my life, but ultimately I made my mother promise me she would feed the baby and I went to the party. I worried about the baby all night, but by the time I got home the next day, the baby rabbit had died.

I felt horrible. I had killed him. He had depended on me, and I had betrayed him with negligence and self-centeredness. Years later I picked up a book in the library that explained what to feed wild babies. First of all, the book warned that almost no babies found in the wild are truly abandoned and the best approach is always to go away and leave them alone so their mother can come back for them. The book rephrased this thought in several different ways, stressing the point. Nonetheless, when I reached the part about feeding baby bunnies I learned that if my neglect had not killed him, what I was feeding him would have. This knowledge does not make me a better person, but it has saved me from the temptation to "rescue" any number of apparently abandoned wild babies since then.

I never did get a horse. Shortly after my best friend got hers, I came to appreciate the difference between fiction and fact. Or perhaps I lacked the skill to form that special bond like Alex and the Black. Perhaps you had to spend several months on a desert island with a horse before that special "click" set in. Whatever it was, I met any number of horses during my horse-loving period before I realized I didn't really like them.

I've had better things to do with my adult life than be rejected by rabbits. I've almost always been kept by at least one cat. Cats are very simple. Live by the cat's rules, or you will hear a muffled little "huff" and you will never see the cat again.

From time to time, however, I have been tempted to own a goat. A small goat: a pygmy goat, perhaps. I like the idea of living lawn mowers (they would be so much easier to start). I understand goats are not hard to feed. And if my goat gets bored, I have more than enough nieces and nephews for her to stand on until the mood passes. I think a goat would work for me.

the secret

my mother was a square dance caller. I have no idea
what would possess a woman to subject her children to
such abject humiliation, but she was drunk with power
and delirious from discovering a whole group of people
who willingly paid her to order them around. The fact
that all of her children were hiding in deep, self-dug
holes in the back yard to avoid public ridicule did not
seem to faze her. She may have even suggested we were
being silly. Our mother cared more than she liked to
admit about what the neighbors might think of us — even
neighbors she'd never met — but what our friends
thought . . . she advised us we were fools to even think
about it. We perceived inconsistency in this: she did not.

I should remember more about square dancing than I
do. Perhaps out of spite I've repressed its history. Square
dancing is what all those people in the funny wide skirts
and cowboy shirts were not doing in the movie *Oklahoma!*
In all of the square dances I watched in all of the years my
mother called, I never once saw her dancers run up the
side of a mound of hay and jump off. My mother's club
danced in a little square building on the edge of the 4-H
fairgrounds — the nearest hay mound was clear down by
the horse barns and it was only there during fair week.

The way square dancing was presented in the movies was a big issue for my mother. She knew for a fact that Mel Blanc (the voice of Bugs Bunny) was a square dance caller, so why people in Hollywood couldn't be a hair more accurate in their depictions eluded her.

I don't know how square dancing came to be. Like most things American it is a little like — but not entirely like — various forms of folk dancing from all over Europe. I assume, from the costumes normally worn while doing it, that at least some of its history was touched by the early West. Very likely some stray Puritan found himself out in the West somewhere (nowhere near Oklahoma) and was challenged to combine religious purity, sexual hunger, folk dancing, and the desire to have just a little fun, all to the same music.

Square dancing requires four couples arranged in a square facing each other, men on the left, women on the right of each couple. The couples respond to a series of "calls," or instructions from the caller, the most well-known being the "swing your partner," do-si-do, and allemand left. Done right, square dancing is fun and very precise: done wrong, it is an awkward and miserable experience that involves running into each other on the dance floor and rushing to get where you think you should be. (There is even an official square dance term for a complete snafu in square dancing — it's called a breakdown.) Gym teachers, in particular, could strip all of the fun from a square dance and turn it into a joyless mess. It must be one of the essay questions on their PE final exam: *describe four ways to make traditional dancing the most hated segment of your students' entire phys ed experience.*

I grew up with square dancers congregating at my house at odd hours of the night, with a mother who went out in public wearing three-tiered gathered skirts fluffed over huge crinolines and fitted blouses with puffy sleeves. And ricrac. Yards and yards and yards of ricrac. (For the unexposed, ricrac is a decorative cloth tape shaped like a zigzag that can be sewn to clothing to make it appear more festive. It has never been fashionable in my lifetime.) And just in case there might be a single individual in town who didn't know whose mother she was, she wore the nametag ELOISE PECK with shadow figures swinging and the name of her club embossed on it. Even worse, there was a certain status to be had (among themselves) for wearing a nametag for every dance club they had ever danced with, so many dancers looked like they could not remember their own names from one tag to the next.

My mother was well suited to be a square dance caller because she loved music, she loved being in charge, and she was entirely comfortable in front of a crowd. Something in my mother needed to rise above the role of everywoman, and being one of very few women callers in her day seemed to help fill that need. In the past few years I have discovered that years of watching my mother in front of groups of people, and remembering what she told me she had learned from those experiences, has gone a long way toward making me comfortable and at ease in front of groups of people myself. And, truthfully, I too enjoy it. This apple has not fallen that far from the tree.

Life between my mother and me was nowhere near as

serendipitous when I was in eighth grade. Eighth grade itself was enough to curdle the teenage soul. Exactly at that stage of life when our feet tripped over thin air and our faces broke out when we inhaled, when body parts were growing where nothing had grown before and the most attractive among us looked like we had been stitched together from spare parts, gym became a required course. Hormonal meltdowns in the locker room were not all that uncommon. And forget about gym class itself; most of us had never before had the opportunity to shower naked in one communal room with thirty-five snippy, insecure, hopelessly judgmental peers. The only way to get out of this growth experience was to tell the gym teacher we were having our period—not yet a confession we made openly or easily. This experience was so anxiety-inducing for some of my classmates that their bodies threw them into perpetual menses. They apparently flowed nonstop for the next five years.

The first thing we did in gym class was get publicly weighed and measured, and that pretty much cured me of gym right there. In my recollection I was the heaviest girl in my class (I was also within a quarter of an inch of being the tallest), but I may just have been the heaviest girl stupid enough to admit to what I weighed. Although size had become a serious emotional issue for me by then, photographs of me at that age show a healthy, outgoing adolescent. Not a stick by any means, but also nothing remotely comparable to my mental body image. I survived it.

I survived calisthenics and fitness evaluations. I survived archery, which, in spite of the teacher's instructions, still resulted in my shaving off the inside of my left arm. And then the gym teacher announced that the next segment of our class was going to be "dance."

It can be difficult for a fourteen-year-old to equate dance with physical education. Ten years later even a fairly fit individual can see an immediate link, but fourteen-year-olds are fairly loose-jointed and flexible. Even pudgy, rhythm-impaired teenagers are apt to break out in fits of dancing in the course of a normal day—it just comes with the hormonal power surges and a culture that identifies itself through music. Dancing, to a fourteen-year-old, means coming into direct and humiliating contact with the opposite sex. It is also readily apparent to a teenager that nothing cool and socially relevant to them will ever be taught in a junior high gym class. The dance segment in gym meant being watched by everyone you know while you are publicly stumbling through the Hokey Pokey.

It was at that point that the gym teacher pulled me to one side and said, "Your mother teaches square dancing, doesn't she? Do you think she would come in and teach the class?" Which is a little like asking someone to arrange the details of their own execution.

My mother was a stay-at-home mom until my youngest brother was born and I was twelve. Then in fairly rapid succession my father lost his job and my mother had our Baby Brother and then went to work. I had hoped that my mother would be far too busy with her new job to come teach my gym class how to square dance, but as luck would have it it was considered important for parents to meddle in their children's education and my mother agreed to come.

Being a caller's kid had a few quirks of its own before this event. The one that always amused me personally were the little notes we found written on the margins of telephone messages or spare paper scraps. Artists doodle, writers jot down particularly clever phrases, musicians write down sequences of music notes . . . square dance callers scribble the never-ending travels of a couple named L(eft) and R(ight). While there are four sets and eight people in a square, the caller often only needs to keep track of set 1. In traditional square dancing set 1 goes to "visit" sets 2, 3, and 4; in Western-style square dancing, all four sets are often doing the same thing, or sets 1 and 2 are interacting while sets 3 and 4 are doing the same thing. L and R danced all over every spare sheet of paper in our house, little circles drawn around the one who was moving and arrows drawn to show where s/he had gone.

It was not uncommon to walk into our house in the course of our own normal business to find our mother "practicing," and when we walked by she would grab us, inform us we were either R or L, and then propel us wherever she wanted us to go. We would find ourselves square dancing with six imaginary people, do-si-do-ing around spots in the rug, promenading with empty hands while she determined whether the sequence of calls she was writing would get the "eight" of us where we all needed to be. (She, on the other hand, found it alarming that so many of *my* friends were imaginary.)

Because she was the club caller, she was responsible for providing the sound system and all of the music. She often encouraged at least one of us to go with her if only to help her carry the equipment. Once there, if an odd number of couples showed up, we would be paired off with our dad and shoved out onto the floor. Once or twice a year the club would have a family night when everyone brought their kids and Mom would call a few simple dances so we could participate.

Because square dancing requires people in sets of four, whenever members of her dance club wanted to bring a new couple they immediately needed three more. The club actively recruited new members, eventually by offering classes that my mother taught, but they also dressed their children up in Western dancewear and had us perform demonstrations, whether on parade floats or in booths, for instance, at the county fair. I had several square dance outfits during the course of my childhood, at least two of which were exact replicas of dresses my mother wore. I rarely told friends at school about any of these activities, but I knew a secret about square dancing that I could not have expected them to know.

So my mother, with her turntable, speakers, monitor, microphone, and a case of 45-rpm records, appeared at my school to teach all of my peers how to square dance. The boys' and the girls' gym classes were combined, and we were paired off and assigned to our squares. All over the gym floor classmates were glancing at me and then laughing at themselves.

The secret is that, taught right by a caller who knows what s/he is doing, square dancing is fun. Each dancer has exactly enough time to get to the next place s/he is supposed to be. It is precise, it's smooth, it flows very gracefully, the music is uptempo and infectious, the dancers are moving just fast enough to get the adrenaline going and not so fast they feel rushed. My mother may have had a natural aptitude for math and therefore could not see why math might be hard for her child, but she had been teaching square dancing for years: she knew how to break it down for beginners, she knew how to stay just ahead of her class, she knew when to tell a joke, when to add an encouraging word. The class she taught went quickly, most of my classmates were surprised to realize they had had fun, and more than one of them came up to me later to tell me that my mother was "cool."

In junior college I was required to take two phys ed courses. I took swimming (I float like a cork, and while I have never been recruited for the Olympics, it would probably require effort to drown me) and a folk dance class. For my class project, I wrote, taught, and called a square dance. I felt, at the time, that I all but cheated, since rather than learning anything new, I simply fell back on knowledge I already had. The square dance went well. My dancers enjoyed themselves. I gave the record back to my mom, and beyond the occasional outbreak of the Hokey Pokey, I have never danced since.

Browsing through the Internet, I discovered that the club my mother called for for twenty-five years, the Coldwater Merry Mixers, still exists. Square dancing seems to be doing well. There are even gay clubs listed under their own heading. Every now and then I'll hear a song over the radio—most often country and western— and I catch myself thinking, *Mom could use that for a square dance.*

chin hair

recently i heard a quote that put vanity in a positive light and I promised myself I would remember it — but that was over an hour ago, so it's long gone now. I'm beginning to believe I've been pulling my short-term memory out of my head through the hairs on my chin.

I do remember the first time I glanced at my reflection and discovered a strand of baling wire hanging from my chin. I was horrified. I grabbed a pair of pliers and yanked it out. I spent days worrying over what anomaly in my body might have caused that to occur, but I was distracted by the discovery of another one. And another.

These were not the ordinary fur that we all grow, nor even those wiry, kinky little bits of fencing that sprout up out of moles: these were thick, feisty, virile poles that jut out and scratch unwary snugglers.

Beardwork.

Furthermore, they were vindictive. It would appear they *object* to being torn out by force. They grow back immediately — often the same day — but they reverse themselves when they come to the flesh line, and start growing back inward toward the brain.

I am convinced that it is the wayward, retro-growing chin hair that leads to memory loss. They seem to happen about the same time. Memory cells are very close to the surface of the brain. Certainly if a gentle tap on the skull with a ball bat can cause memory loss, the steady, stubborn excavation of ingrown chin hairs could have the same effect.

If only I had not stopped to pluck the forest along my jawline, I might know where my car keys are right now.

i am in shape. My shape is round.

When I was younger I imagined with every new day that I was on the cusp of developing a lifelong habit of physical fitness. The developmental stage of this habit has turned out to be uncommonly long, but at the time I believed it, body and soul. I was suffering a minor lapse of self-indulgence, and any minute now a burst of resolve would drive me to the gym or an exercise machine and—within a matter of weeks, perhaps, or at the very most, months—I would reclaim that fit and youthful figure that was mine.

The fact that my fit and youthful figure was borrowed from five years of actual physical labor in a factory, or that the pounds began adding back on almost from the day I left that job neither dampened my enthusiasm nor daunted my faith. For about three years of my life I was thin(ner), strong, and able to walk long miles without a single huff, and nothing but basic intrinsic laziness was keeping me from being thin and strong again. It was a matter of will.

As it happens, the fitness challenge in my life dove-tailed very nicely with my passion for buying things. I bought fitness machines. I bought rowers and bicycles and weights and stationary bikes, I bought jogging shoes and exercise outfits and sweatpants and little stretchy wrist- and headbands. I bought gym memberships. I bought exercise classes. It is truly a shame the body does not tally up and award points for the effort it takes just to gather the things that will help us get into shape.

Back when I was so persistently chasing the ideal, however, my shape was just more or less "bulgy." Exercise outfits made me look fat. Attempting to exercise made me look awkward and stiff and red in the face. All of it—breathing itself—made me sweat.

It was about this time that I would come home from work, wriggle my jellyrolls into yet another stretchy exercise outfit, and slog off to class. Usually the entire incentive to go was the dinner I planned to eat on the way home. Still, I knew, as soon as the exercise gene kicked in and I really got *into* the program, I too would learn to look at food as mere fuel, and not as the reward. I would come home from my exercise program feeling fit and strong and morally virtuous and stiff as a board, and my back porch light would be on.

I never turned on the back porch light.

When I bought the house, I saw that porch and I thought to myself, *A weaker person would allow this room to fill up with all of the things they don't use.* I resolved never to do that.

Five years later the back porch held the litterbox and six pieces of exercise equipment.

I hardly ever went out there.

I had no reason to turn on the back porch light.

And yet, there the light would be, beaming for all to see . . .

I would stand there, fondling the string, and wonder to myself, *Exactly how did this light get on?*

I even asked the cat, but he had no apparent opinion. The cat—Babycakes—was at the time about six months old. He was a gorgeous kitten, a red tabby—an unusually fluffy red tabby, for a short-haired cat—but he had never possessed quite the cuddly, sweet disposition I had tried to impose on him with his name. Someone less bent on filling her own needs with catflesh would have named him "Digger," or perhaps "Hellspawn": I wanted a lap cat, a pick-up-and-cuddle cat, so I named him Babycakes. And I can pick him up and cuddle him. I routinely warn others not to even try it, and I keep bandages on hand for the hard-of-believing, but he *looks* for all the world like a big old long-haired pick-him-up-and-cuddle cat.

During the random dawnings of the light Babycakes was still small and oddly haired, and every now and then his back end overran his front end and dumped him in clumsy heaps on the linoleum. He was barely as tall as my ankle. At odd moments of the day or night he might turn into a faint pink streak that galloped from one end of the house to the other, making more noise in transit than the average dump truck.

I was standing in the kitchen one night after exercise class. Perhaps I was trying to bring normal color back to my face. A faint pink streak roared through the kitchen, out onto the porch, vaulted onto the exercise bike, crawled like an inchworm up onto the bike seat, s-t-re-t-c-h-e-d his fine gold self between the seat and the handlebars, and began batting savagely at the light string. By the third swat, the light came on. The cat fell off the bike, shook himself off, and sauntered out of the kitchen as if to say, "So *there*."

Occasionally guests would come to my house, admire my decor, and laugh when they saw my exercise bike on the back porch. "So this is where you work out?" they might tease.

"Actually," I would answer, "we use it to turn on the light."

And they would stand there, looking at my bike. Occasionally the more curious might reach out and just experimentally touch the light string, as if expecting some sort of invisible challenge.

The cat would walk over to his dish and sniff.

my grandmother molby was probably in her sixties when she began her life as a nomad. I believe she was driven off her farm (belatedly) by the Great Depression, or the fear of the next coming depression, or the election of a Democratic president—whatever compelled her, sometime in the mid-1950s my grandmother packed up my grandfather and all of their worldly goods, left the farm where they had lived for thirty or forty years, and went house-shopping.

When my grandmother moved (and I presume it was my grandmother who moved—once she made up her mind something was going to happen she had a gift for "fussing" about it until all opposition got out of her way) she moved everything they owned. She moved the Victrola, which she stored in the new barn across the road. She moved the solid brass bed that she later sold to an antique dealer for five dollars, she moved the marble-top tables that she sold to the same man, she moved the artwork she had done as a child . . . she moved everything. My grandmother survived the Great Depression: she was not a woman to throw anything away.

They could not have moved because the house was too big or the farm too hard to manage, because they moved to a bigger house on a bigger farm out on M-86, west of town. While I remember their house on Michigan Avenue (and there are photographs of me as a child taken all around it), it is the house on M-86 that I associate with my grand-mother. It was a big old two-story house with weathered shake siding, a big, long stone porch, and some of the most beautiful woodwork I have ever seen. It had pillared, built-in bookshelves between the living room and the dining room. It had a glorious staircase. It had bay windows in the dining room. It had a see-through wooden china cabinet with cut-glass windows as the wall between the kitchen and the dining room. It had forced steam-heat baseboard heating that always sounded, when I slept upstairs alone, like Jack the Ripper was coming for me up the stairs. It had four bedrooms upstairs, but my grandparents immedi-ately built a bedroom and bath for themselves on the main floor. In the upstairs bathroom there was a claw-foot tub I could climb into for my bath and I could barely see over the sides. I loved the house on M-86.

Between two big cement gateposts there was the lane that went back to the back fields of the farm. This was a two-lane dirt road, perfect for exercising my imaginary horses. I fought many fierce battles of the Wild West on that road. When I went to my grandmother's house I spent hours under the pignut tree probably half a mile from the house. I battled evil or was evil, depending on my mood at the time. I robbed banks and trains, held up saloons, fought with noble Indians, and hanged myself without mercy. I was a self-entertaining child: it was not the absence of other children my age that ever caused me problems when I was a kid.

When I wasn't racing up and down the lane, I was sequestered upstairs in the privacy of an old saloon hotel. The upstairs was uncommonly suited to that fantasy because the stairway came up the back wall and then circled around, and the hallway was open, the railing looking back down the stairway—just like an old Western hotel on television. My grandmother must have gone up there, because there was never so much as a dust mote anywhere, but she left me to my own amusements when I was staying with her.

Very little of the time I spent with my grandparents was spent with either one of them. My grandmother routed my grandfather out of bed at 7:30 every morning (it was time to make the bed) and he would dress, shave, have breakfast, and then go take a nap in his rocker in the living room. If I happened to wander through before he had dozed off he would have me sit down and then he would regale me with tales of the railroad. He worked for the railroad all through the Depression. He was a professional train rider. He had started out in a different position, but as the Depression dragged on and more and more people were laid off he was bumped from one job to another until finally his job consisted of getting on the trains and riding from here to there to somewhere else (he knew all of these places by name) and then in a week or two coming home. This was apparently a nuisance, and he was glad when the Depression was over. He used words like "the Chesapeake and Ohio" or "the Nickelplate," Baltimore, Washington, D.C., Gary, and Chicago. His voice reminded me of Clark Gable, so almost anything he said *sounded* significant, but his ramblings about the trains and working for the railroad were the most boring lectures I had heard in my short life. I would be a near adult before I would reason that if people paid to ride the trains, it was unlikely the railroad had hired my grandfather to do it.

The house on M-86 was a beautiful house, but it was hard on my grandmother's nerves. They lived there for twelve years, and survived eleven traffic accidents in their front yard. Headed west on M-86, approaching my grandmother's house there was a sharp curve that was improperly graded and required a certain attention to detail to navigate. Late at night, coming home from the bars, drunks in particular piled into the cement post at the end of the lane, or climbed one of the two trees in the front yard with their car, or missed her yard but wound up across the street (also her property) in front of the barn. One missed all of the other obstacles and ran across her lawn and into her stone porch. Adventures like these were simply another attraction for us kids, but our grandmother became convinced that sooner or later someone was going to get killed, and she couldn't bear it. (We all wanted to be there.) She was also acutely aware of how long it took the ambulance to reach her house, and she worried about my grandfather's heart. I don't know that there was anything wrong with my grandfather's heart, but she was never one to stanch a worry when she could just as easily fuss. Eventually she decided to move him into town, where he would be closer to the hospital.

To achieve this end, she began "sorting." Out went the brass bedstead. Out went the marble-top tables. My grandmother owned a lot of beautiful old antique furniture, but she was not a strong admirer of antiques, and since they meant little to her, they were not, in her estimation, worth very much. I, on the other hand, was raised by people who fondled the grain of their wood, who looked for those little wooden blocks in the corners of drawers (they mean something), who admired dovetailing and quartersawn oak and bird's-eye maple—I have never liked modern furniture.

And I have always loved music. Hidden safely in the corner of an unused haymow was my Grandmother Molby's old Victrola. It worked. It had 78s, it had extra needles. The sound was a little scratchy, but there must have been easily twenty records. To run it, I had to wind it up by hand, and when it began to wear down, it played slower. It was roughly four feet tall and perhaps two feet square. It was made out of polished walnut—the cabinet alone was beautiful.

My grandmother decided it was "worthless" and needed to go to the dump.

I begged. I cried. I pleaded. I wanted it, and I wanted it badly.

My mother noted that I didn't have anywhere to put it. I noted that I lived in a room that was 14-by-14 and hardly cramped.

My grandmother said, "You don't want that dirty old thing."

I established I did want it. I offered to clean it up, although I couldn't see what was "dirty" about it. I gave it my best shot. And I was not a stupid child: I knew it was a collector's item, I knew it stood a good chance of being worth good money someday.

But my grandmother had decreed it "dirty" and dirt is the kiss of death.

"You don't *need* it," my mother said, knowing full well who could fuss the hardest the longest and the most.

And off the Victrola went to the dump.

The house on M-86 is still there. The orchard is gone. Someone enclosed the stone porch with aluminum and sided the house with pale green aluminum siding. Every now and then my Beloved and I drive by it on our way to family reunions and she sticks her fingers in her ears as we go around the last curve. *I don't think it's* *"godawful green,"* she's been known to say. *Perhaps they own it and they can paint it any color they want.* Browsing through old photographs recently I found a picture of the house on M-86 in all of its old glory, which I showed to her triumphantly. "This is what it *used* to look like," I crowed.

"Well, it doesn't now," my Beloved replied cheerfully.

It's not true that I have a hard time letting go of the past. From time to time I go to antique shows and I stop and price the rare Victrolas I find there. I just like to know what being the least stubborn of three generations of women cost me.

winter kill

The crocus are back
braving the cold,
their single efficient stem
jabbing skyward, their single
efficient bloom curled gently
around their sex.
Crocus are tough plants.

Last year
the crocus were blooming
as I stood on the river's edge
where Dan put his garden,
dead leaves and blooming crocus
under my feet, the river racing
with all of spring's fury
below me. He lived
in such a wild and beautiful
place.

It was a hard winter
for AIDS patients.
These are not Dan's crocus
and this is not Dan's garden
and this spring
Dan will not be coming back.

boxes in the attic

when i was a little girl — five, perhaps — one of my mother's friends from high school stopped by our house on her way home from church. I had no idea my mother had any friends before me so I was fascinated, but I was quickly shunted outside to "play" with her daughter. I don't remember anything about this child except she was wearing a white dress, and I only remember that because it got me into trouble. Our family did not go to church. I never wore white dresses on Sunday (or any other day of the week, if I could help it). To amuse the daughter of my mother's friend as I had been directed, I invited her to climb down under the back porch and visit my new puppies. They were wonderful puppies as I recall. Six of them, all different variations of black-and-white mutt. Each one of them had a name because I was a responsible and dedicated puppy-keeper. My intentions were unsullied. My motives were pure. Unfortunately, the black dirt under our back porch was neither, and the resulting damage to that white dress was blamed not on the little girl wearing it but on me.

Who understands the logic that runs through a small child's mind? By the time I was six something dark and hideously wrong had tangled itself around my soul. (Not necessarily as a direct result of the puppy incident.) I believed I was bad. Not just mildly bad, not just poorly behaved at times: I believed the very core of my being was rotten, that there was nothing that would fix it, nothing that could make it better. This belief in congenital, inextricable baseline evil followed me through my childhood and into my early adulthood. It automatically negated anything good or positive or supportive anyone might say about me and it dwelled obsessively on even the slightest hint of moral defect. I believed that no one loved me. I believed that no one loved me because I was inherently evil and did not deserve to be loved. If they did love me, it was only because they did not know me well enough. *If you really knew me . . .* Most of my childhood was spent wading through dark and endless interior monologues about not being loved, not being understood, not being worthy of love or understanding.

It was my fault the little girl's dress got dirty. It was my fault I threw a rock and hit my kid sister in the head. It was my fault my parents argued or I got sick and they didn't know how to pay for a doctor or I asked for something that was frivolous and foolish when there were other people in the family to think about. My parents reminded me almost daily of how irresponsible and self-ish I could be, while I recall my childhood as one of just endless, unrelenting responsibility. And I was not worthy. I was not strong enough to hold my world together. A better child might have been, but I was not that better child. I was the bad child. A failure.

I was also a fat child. I was too tall for my age, clumsy and awkward. I remember sitting at the kitchen table trying to eat my lunch while my mother told me how miserable her life as a fat child had been, how miserable mine would be when I moved into junior and senior high. I had the power right now, she told me, to change my life as she had not been able to do: and if I failed, kids would tease me even more than they already had. Boys would never like me. The cool kids would ignore me. She wanted to spare me that humiliation, my mother would affirm as she burst into tears. All she ever wanted was for me to be happy. Somehow not only my size but also my failure to find happiness was added to my long list of personal defects.

Somewhere in the fantasy that passes for greater truth there is the Perfect Child in a white dress who never gets dirty, who never uses bad words, who sits with her knees together and her hands folded neatly in her lap. She is the child I never was and the child I should have aspired to be. She is the child so perfect that even when she does get dirty it is not her fault. I never wanted to be her. Hell, at her age I didn't even want to be a *girl*, much less a well-behaved, well-mannered, excruciatingly clean girl. Still, she existed, the model against which I was judged and against which I have never measured up.

It is amazing what we find buried in old boxes in the attic. I had forgotten all about her. I had forgotten I ever even cared.

But I did.

—

Apparently I still do.

This spring a long-lost friend reappeared in my Beloved's life. "You have to meet her," my Beloved said

cheerfully, eager to share with me her glow of reconcili-
ation, and so the three of us met. Her friend—we can call
her Susan—is about five feet four. She has blond hair.
Blue eyes. She is a size six. She is bright and entertaining and a person for whom appearances are obviously
important. This is my judgment, not hers.

Appearances are important to all of us: we have
varying standards of how we need to appear and what
we expect of others, no one standard superior or inferior
to any other. And the problem that arises between Susan
and me is not what Susan expects of me, but of what I
presume Susan expects of me—I have a stuck throttle
when it comes to what I call "little people." The fact that
Susan and my Beloved were childhood friends, the fact
that their relationship has been through any number of
transformations . . . none of that bothers me. What bothers me is that Susan is small and cute and blond and she
is my enemy.

She is the little girl in the white dress who was so
perfect that it was my fault her dress got dirty.

I expect that was not the lesson my mother wanted
me to take away from that event. I expect she was just
trying to teach me to stop and think. My instincts tell me
she was embarrassed when her friend's previously
immaculate daughter came crawling out of the black dirt
under our back porch. I would imagine at that moment
comparisons between the two children present would
have been inevitable.

And it is not that that particular event was remarkable
to me at the time, or even later, so much as it seems to sym-
bolize what was wrong with me and how I lost my right-

ful place in the world. It identified for me an enemy. Someone I could blame for what I felt I'd lost, however vague and ill-defined in my own mind that "loss" might be.

It is exactly the same thought process that results in racism or sexism or ageism. I am a sizist. I, who lobby endlessly (at least in my heart) for the equal rights of people of size, am predisposed to distrust "little people." I expect they will judge me harshly. I expect they will reject me. I approach relationships with them with carefully guarded expectations and one foot perpetually aimed for the door. *You can't trick me into liking you— I know what you really think about me.*

In truth, Susan has never been anything but kind to me. In truth, if Susan weighed forty more pounds I would probably embrace her as an equal. This is not a characteristic I admire about myself. Nor is it one that follows any true line of logic. I have known women of size who are more critical of other women of size than any small, "perfectly" shaped woman would ever think to be. And I have known small, delicately shaped women who never think about size much, one way or the other.

At some point in my life I looked at my reflection and I said to the person standing there, *Suppose this is all there is? Suppose this "temporary" weight gain of ten or fifteen years never meets that long-anticipated burst of dieting self-discipline? Suppose you are going to spend the rest of your life fat? Do you want to spend your life fat and miserable? Or could you convince yourself you are a self-loving woman of size?*

And if all you ever changed in your life was your attitude about it, whose goddamned business is it anyway?

I am not advocating obesity as a lifestyle. I am advocating the serenity prayer as a path to inner peace.

Still, I have the moral obligation to change what I can change. There is a box in my personal attic that I do not need, some old, malformed chunk of personal history that has turned musty with age and has become ugly and counterproductive and hurtful just by being. I need to go up there and do some serious cleaning. Dust off all of the old boxes so I can see what lies inside, throw out what I don't need, take better care of what I do . . . It's a lifelong habit, maintaining an attic, and one I tend from time to time to let go.

I need to find that little girl in the white dress and forgive her. As she is a part of all of us, she is a long-neglected part of me. It was not her fault. She didn't do anything wrong. I suppose I could continue to punish her for the rest of my life, but if I can find it within myself to seek forgiveness, the first step surely must be to forgive.

doorknob boxing

my beloved and i have friends who are in transition. All relationships are in transition, I suppose, but our friends are struggling to consolidate two lives and two different towns and all of the accoutrements of middle age into one joint partnership. There are several stumbling blocks to this process, but the one my Beloved and I can relate to immediately is the cat. There is an unwritten rule in the universe that those of us who truly love our cats will fall in love with a potential life partner with an incurable, unbearable allergy to cat dander. Our friends, one allergic, one catted, have decided to create a cat-free space within their home.

To the best of my knowledge — and I have done some extensive research — there is no way to separate a cat from its dander without irreparably harming the cat. One of the true beauties of the cat is the shape of the cat, and as anyone who has ever accidentally gotten their cat wet immediately realizes, the shape of the cat is the shape of the coat of the cat. Remove or damage the coat of a cat and the pathetic misshapen being left will be so ashamed it will dash into the kitchen and immediately impale itself on a carving knife. Cats know what makes them beautiful and mysterious and correctly shaped. This is why any self-respecting cat is almost always grooming himself.

I grew up in the country surrounded by farms. Farms are where the combination of grain storage and grain-consuming rodents brought about the relationship between cats and humans. I was raised by a cat—Gus— who was born and bred on a farm. A farmer gave her to my father when she was just a kitten. She rode all day with him in his fuel oil delivery truck, delicately sharing his lunch with him at noon, and he brought her into the house and introduced her to my mother. Gus accepted my mother as hairless but possibly useful, said, "Excuse me," and went out to the kitchen to kill a mouse. She ruled our home for eleven years, and because spending money on free pets was a conundrum for my parents, Gus was free to roam and free to tend to her reproductive instincts. I clearly remember evenings when Gus would be on our back porch, telling my mother quite emphatically that she needed to GO OUTSIDE while my mother would be imitating cat calls for the six or seven frustrated males already out there. As a result of her wanton ways, Gus was almost always either pregnant or raising kittens, and I grew up with a never-ending supply of cats.

I have almost always lived with a cat.

It is the basis of this life experience that has led me to smile, nod, and maintain a discreet silence while our friends explain their plans to create a cat-free space for the more allergic of the two of them. This plan involves a French door, a louvered door, and a fireplace screen.

I have to be honest: there is no evidence to suggest so

far that their plan will not work. The fireplace screen is set in place at the base of the stairway. Apparently the first time the cat (Simon) saw this screen he said to himself, "This can't possibly have anything to do with me," and he jumped over it. As he jumped his hind feet hit the screen, which teetered and wobbled and crashed to the floor with a clatter that so thoroughly destroyed his nerves that he has never gone near it again. He has erased the entire upstairs of the house from his mind. When his people go up there he never so much as wonders where they've gone, he just yawns and wanders out to the kitchen to check to make sure they filled his food bowl.

I have heard comments to suggest that the French doors are not as frightening to him. Still—so far—the plans seems to work. There are catted areas of the house, and there are cat-free areas of the house, and the cat seems to respect these barriers being established in this, his ninth year of rule in this house.

My Beloved is violently allergic to cats. Her throat swells and grows hives. The whites of her eyes turn pink and begin to swell out of their sockets. She sniffles, her eyes leak sticky fluids. Her asthma kicks in and you can hear her trying to breathe several rooms away. She has spent a great deal of our together time at my house on the front steps, or in a tent out behind the house.

I live with one cat. Babycakes. Babycakes is a long-haired red tabby. There are hairs on this cat that measure as much as three inches. He appears to grow these hairs in about 7.2 minutes, and when one falls out he grows two to replace it. In a week and a half he can completely carpet a hardwood floor. He grows fine red/gold fuzz that looks more like angel hair or angora yarn than cat hair. He was twelve years old in March. He is in perfect health. He is twelve pounds of walking, breathing, shedding cat dander, and proud of it.

In the beginning my Beloved and I discussed the possibilities of sharing a home. We considered marking off certain areas to be "cat-free." At this time I lived in Jackson, she lived in Three Rivers, and the hour-and-a-half drive between the two had become tiresome. As a sort of trial run we decided—for reasons having nothing to do with allergies or cat maintenance—to spend about an hour or so alone in my bedroom, cat-free. Having already discovered the joys of trying to leap off a waterbed swiftly and gracefully in order to detach the cat from the flaming candle toasting his belly hair, we opted for a little alone time.

We closed the bedroom door.

The door popped right back open like the knob was attached to a rubber band and an indignant red tabby marched into the room, looked me square in the eye, and said, "Did you realize someone *closed the door*?" And he looked askance at my Beloved.

I escorted him outside, shut the door, and propped her sixty-pound suitcase against it.

We smiled triumphantly at each other. We were alone.

And we remained alone for a good hour and a half.

Perhaps the longest hour and a half either of us have ever spent, but . . .

First a small gold paw snaked under the door and dug around for something to hang on to.

Then he spoke to me.

Then he cried.

Then he expressed anger, outrage, humiliation, heartbreak, betrayal, and brokenheartedness.

Then he took up doorknob boxing.

I have no idea what doorknob boxing looks like from Babycakes' side of the door: all I know was it was an old knob and it was not all that firmly established in its hole, and as a result as the cat boxed with the knob the whole door quivered and rattled and begged for mercy. A platoon of marines charging up the stairs in full combat gear could not have made any more noise. A herd of firemen ramming the door with a battering ram would not have been more distracting. I swear the house began to shake in sympathy.

It took him an hour and a half of hammering, but he managed to move a sixty-pound suitcase and an eight-foot door with the sheer strength of his will. He got the door open a quarter of an inch, and then, as cats do, he flattened himself to the width of a sheet of paper and willed himself into the room. We played *Here, let me put my cold, wet little nose in your ear.* We played *I'm so happy to see you/where have you been/did you know someone tried to keep me out of here?* We played *Stomp on the human/knead the head of the human/lick the nose of the human.*

The long and arduous task of breaking through the door had him stoked with adrenaline, and for most of the night he stalked and purred and nuzzled. If he was under the covers he needed immediately to be out, if he was out he needed immediately to burrow in. He was like a toddler on speed; he was overcome with boundless and inexhaustible love and energy. He loved me, he loved my Beloved, he loved every square inch of the room from which he had recently and rudely been exiled.

It was a long night. The cat stomped, while my Beloved sniffled and sneezed and kept saying, "I really think I'm getting better, really—I used to be a *lot* more allergic than this . . ."

The day I met her I lived an hour and a half away and I lived with four cats. At the age of eighteen Jasmine said to me, "*I'm old and I'm tired and I hurt all of the time, and you're never home anymore anyway,*" and she laid down and quietly died. Gypsy, who was eleven, suffered health problems that prevented her from suviving our inevitable move. Neurotic Nick, the closet cat, moved with Babycakes and me, but he never made the transition emotionally, and two years later—then eleven himself—he transitioned right on to the big closet in the sky.

The cat who was three years old when I met my Beloved—the cat I brought home because I had three cats who hated to cuddle, the cat who sets aside most of his nights for passionate cuddling, not caring that I'd rather sleep—that cat is now twelve. A healthy, robust cat still in his prime. He is a character, with more than one personality trait that not just anyone would be willing to live with. My friends all love to hear about him, but so far no one has agreed to give him a new home.

Within a few weeks of the doorknob-boxing incident, my Beloved's mother moved in with her. I transferred my job across the state and bought a house for Babycakes two blocks from where they live. So her mother lives with my Beloved and my cat waits patiently for me to come home, and when people ask I say, "She's allergic to my cat and her mother needs serenity." We discuss other solutions, explore other options, but—today—this is the solution we live with.

trans-scendental meditation

i am sitting here in my computer room on the last day of my vacation because the single strongest driving force behind my creativity is procrastination. In the background, over and over, I am listening to Wynonna Judd belt out the old Foreigner tune "I Want to Know What Love Is." I might tell you that even if it weren't true just to aggravate Wy, bless her homophobic little heart. I am experiencing a little personal kinship with Wynonna just this moment. I thought I had come so far.

First of all, I have never quite extinguished that adolescent drive to be cool. I am pretty much resigned to the unlikelihood of my inner coolness showing through at this late date, but now—exactly as in junior high—I feel compelled to keep my visible uncoolness at an absolute minimum. Some people embrace their freedom as social outcasts and go on to write *South Park*: I have always hovered along the edges of the In Crowd, never really expecting acceptance so much as perhaps momentary acknowledgment. I live to be showered with the brief and inconsequential attentions of the Socially Chosen. My perceptions of who is cool have changed radically over the past fifty-odd years, but my desire to be one of them has never completely gone away.

For the most part I live in two spheres: the realm of my own personal and professional life, and the Michigan Womyn's Music Festival. For me Festival is six days a year when all of the old rules are thrown away. There are, of course, new rules in their place, but I have never had much reason to question those. Festival has always been about tearing down preconceived notions I brought to the land. I have suffered over nudity, open drug use, minor issues of race . . . Each year on the way to Festival we drive past the trans camp, and each year the issue of transgendered womyn flares up and dies down. My closest connection to the struggles of the transgendered has been a postcard someone gave me at the gate.

The first question we ask about a newborn is exactly what it has always been: Is it a boy or a girl? Why do we need to know that? Do we hold boys differently? Do we have different expectations when a male baby cries? I understand that babies are pretty much a blank slate and in the absence of personality, their sex, height, and weight are about the only conversational topics they have to offer . . . Still, try holding a generic baby in your arms without knowing his/her sex. I did it once. When his mother told me he was a boy I realized I had assumed she was a girl—and someone started moving furniture around in my head. My whole attitude toward that baby changed, and while I cannot tell you what the change was, it was necessary and fundamental.

I went to college during the late sixties, early seventies. Everyone had long hair. Everyone dressed like they bought their clothes at the Mission. I wore jeans and an old army jacket all the way through school. About half the store clerks and gas station attendants I met called me "Sir." Ours was an androgynous era, an era that challenged sexism, racism, preassigned sexual roles. Gay dances were held on my campus and were advertised widely enough that even I knew about them. I was curious and I wanted to go (watch the queers) but I could never find anyone to go with me (to protect me from aggressive lesbians). The opportunity to open my eyes and see life through a new light was all around me, words and possibly even ideas seeping into my unconsciousness, but I watched it all through the thick glaze of culture shock.

I embraced feminism because the traditional female role I had been raised around bored me and it was a kick to be around bright, intelligent women who told me it was okay to hate ironing. Once I realized the traditional female role of cooking, cleaning, and having kids was not a mandatory life choice, most of my gender-identity issues cleared right up. I got a job driving a forklift where I could still wear jeans, and it was another five years before the whole issue of why I was unhappy living in Straightville became an issue again.

When I embraced lesbianism I embraced with it a few philosophical misapplications I have been unlearning ever since. Essentially, I gave myself permission to believe that men and Christians are bad. This was incredibly freeing, since most of my conflicts in the world where I lived were with one or the other, but then I met a man I actually liked, and then another, and then I met a Christian man with an ugly gift for calling me on my unenlightened generalizations.

I have pictured my life as that of a flower slowly but steadily unfolding to the beauty and complexity of the universe of ideas.

And then I met a trans. (Isn't that cute? Wouldn't you like to just take me out to the water tank and hold my head under? I met a person who is or was or has been at some point in the process of gender reassignment. She is also very bright, immensely patient, funny, and about four times as well-read as I will ever be, but you'll have to come back to get me because I'm stuck back on *I met a trans* . . .)

I may have to tape my right eyebrow in place: it keeps jumping up into my forehead of its own accord. In (and out of) the company of my new friend I have spent hours challenging not even sexual roles per se, but those subtle, nonverbal cues we give each other that define our sexuality, our intentions, our personal identity to people we have just met. What is it, exactly, that women do when they meet another woman that says, *I am like you.* I'll be frank here—just walking around loose in the world, I can't tell a lesbian from a straight woman, and some young people I can't tell male from female. I have a gay male friend who is the daughter my mother hoped I'd be, I have gay male friends who call their partner "she" . . . You would think that at some point I would just give up the Midwestern down-home-on-the-farm men do the yardwork, women keep the house bullshit and just accept people as people.

I can't. I have to tear my eyes away or I will watch everything she says, every hand motion, every smoothing of her skirt, every picking up of her fork . . . What *is* that? *Excuse me, but I'm the femininity police . . .* It's enough to send me running back to check my flannel collection.

Part of my mind keeps asking me, *Why is this a struggle at all?* She says she's a woman: she's a woman. What special sacred temple do you think she's breaking into anyway?

Because she's not really a woman. After years of battling over the whole notion of a "real man," do I now have to go back and tilt swords at the windmill of the "real woman"? What internalized set of rules qualifies me—of all people—to be the gatekeeper? NO FAUX WOMEN ALLOWED HERE. I'd be lucky if they let me in.

The standard male/female assumptions do not fully accommodate my personality, never mind someone born physically one sex and emotionally another. More importantly, they cannot possibly accommodate my friend's life. *My* sexuality is not that simple: Should I assume that, like me when I threw out all men and Christians with my heterosexuality, she has rejected all things masculine? That there was never anything about being a boy, or being perceived as a boy, that she liked? There is no boy-trained thought process left, there is nowhere any essential part of her self that is anything but female? None of us are all feminine or all masculine. As a child I never wanted to be a girl, but it never once occurred to me to tell anyone I was anything else. However grudgingly, I did all of the things that little girls do. I cannot help but believe my childhood was fundamentally different from that of someone born male and believing his sexuality is just outright wrong—if only because I was born female and she was born male. Because we were held differently as babies.

Knowing how woefully ignorant this must seem, part of me wants to touch my friend lightly on the shoulder and say, "I understand the appeal, I really do—but trust me, if I had had a choice, I would not be a woman. You have no idea the restrictions you are introducing into your life . . ." As if someone born in the wrong body would be clueless about such issues. Perhaps what I am confronting, dealing ostensibly with my new friend, is my own ambivalent attitudes about gender. Or—whoa!—maybe it's that old *You say what?* knee-jerk reaction to radicals:

If I had a choice, I would not be a woman.

Perhaps what my friend is saying to me, simply by being, is, *You had a choice. You always had a choice. Your choice was to adapt. My choice was to change the situation.*

Harrumph.

Transgendered people existed in Native American cultures, where they were respected and often considered healers. They were called "two-spirits." If we are indeed the whole sum of our life experience, I find "two-spirits" easier to deal with than "trans" or "male-to-female" or "female-to-male." My friend always refers to herself as "she," but I understand not all transgendered people treasure such consistency. And why should they? Their lives have been mostly potluck—why should those of us who interact with them get off easy?

I have not reached a single conclusion anywhere in this. I do not want to embarrass my new friend, who has been very kind to me. I have never been a person who embraces a new idea until I discover it printed on the grille of an oncoming truck, while my friend has shown courage and the willingness to remain open in situations that are all but incomprehensible to me. I do not know her well enough to sit down and say, "Okay, I have some questions," nor do I assume it is her responsibility to educate me.

Still, it seems clear someone has to talk to that person who is moving all of that furniture around in my head. It's hard to look cool while an armoire is sliding around behind your eyes.

coyote

Late evening lit in fading gold
a coyote trotted across the road
fox-tailed
too skinny for a dog
he bounded along the tree rows as if
his back feet were on springs,
then—sensing I had stopped—he stopped
looking back, feral eyes suspicious
cautious
unafraid:
and we stood there, predator eyeing predator,
hunters acknowledging like souls.
I thought, *You should not be here.*

I live in a nearly perfect world where I am always safe,
in a nation obsessed with protecting its young,
a nation where all sharp corners are padded,
all steep drops have guardrails
and all dangerous steps are clearly marked,
where all feral predators who could pose a threat
to human life are gone.
We cannot have coyotes just
running loose, here.

Watching the coyote, sensing the hunter rise
within me, I felt a jolt of recognition

wild meeting wild.

We have not come all that far, yet.

We have forgotten who we are,
and we do horrible things to those most like us
in our forgetting.

We are hunters protecting our food source.

Nothing less
Nothing more.

tomboy

i was a tomboy as a kid. To look at me now you might not know that, but I was. My best friend was a tomboy, and I was determined to be everything that my best friend might want me to be. It's possible I might even have played with dolls to impress her, but fortunately neither my loyalties nor my backbone were put to that sort of test.

I was tough and rugged and (when my mother wasn't around) I used bad words. As it happens I was about half-feral anyway, so I had a number of qualities that worked on my enemies without my full understanding of exactly why. For instance, I gained a sudden, inexplicable popularity when the kickball season opened on the playground. Classmates who had ignored or avoided me all year suddenly wanted me on their team. Everyone in school seemed to know I was a serious and respected kicker, although I swear I only kicked one classmate, back in third grade. He asked for it. In fact, after I kicked him the first time, he stood there, and he looked at me, and he said, "Do it again."

It is possible he conjured up this approach all on his own, but I suspect he had sought the subtle guidance of an adult. I suspect he had complained to some nonparenting, nonteaching adult, and he had explained he didn't want to appear to be a sissy or whatever by turning me in, but his shins were in mortal peril (okay, I may have kicked him more than once). He couldn't hit me back, I'm sure he explained to this adult, because I was a girl, but I was a girl with one hell of a kick and he secretly feared the breaking of bones in his immediate future. This adult—clouded as he/she was by adult thinking—then foolishly said to my victim, "Use shame—make her realize how cruel she is for hurting you, make her realize you have twice the courage she has because you can Take It." Into each life, I suppose, some really bad advice shall fall.

I kicked him again. I never even stopped to ask myself why he might want that. I probably would have stood there and kicked him until either I got tired or I hurt my foot, because empathy was not my strong suit and because a willing, even eager victim was just too good to pass up. But my best friend got bored watching me kick this kid and dragged me off on a new adventure.

I don't remember where the boy with the flagrant shins came from. He may have been in my third grade class—or perhaps he was in my best friend's class—but I don't remember him hanging around much until about fourth grade. He came from an odd family—perhaps his mother was dead, or he had a stepmother—and he swore to me, on a stack of Bibles, that he had false teeth. I never completely believed him, but I never completely disbelieved him, either, and my curiosity kept the subject popping back up. He swore his teeth were false, but he refused to take them out to show me. I would consult with my best friend, *Do you think he REALLY has false teeth?* But she lacked my passion for absolute truth. She would shrug, as if it didn't matter. "Who cares?" she would ask, although I thought the answer to that should have been glaringly obvious.

And I don't remember why the boy with possibly false teeth and flagrant shins hung around us so often. He was there every recess, lurking on the fringes of our games, breaking into our conversations with bursts of masculine brilliance so socially adept and clever that for a while we thought he had a false brain.

I kicked him during recess because I was a horse, and this is what horses do. He seemed to accept this with a sort of stoic endurance. I sometimes had the impression he would have tolerated anything from us, as long as we let him hang around, but I never had any conception of what that might mean. I was in fourth grade and too young to have heard the word "masochist," and I was too close to my former life as a kindergarten pariah to assume—or even consider—that he might like me. I probably assumed he liked my best friend, which made him no friend of mine. I liked to keep her circle of friends just as small and as tight as I could, so she would have ample opportunity to appreciate me. She may have been casual about who liked her and who didn't, but I had not yet evolved to that level of serene indifference. I held on to those few friends I had with both hands.

All I really know is that I left bruises the size of half-dollars on that poor boy's shins, but I have no memory of his being unkind or even unfriendly toward me. I have no clear sense of what my motives may have been. I may have been jealous. I may have felt threatened. I suspect it was not even that deep.

I think I did it for all of the best reasons a bully does anything. Because either in fact, or merely within the perceptions of my own mind, I felt that someone had done it to me, and I wanted to get even.

I did it because I could.

This is not to imply that all tomboys are bullies, or that there is even any direct connection between the two. Some of us are born to the roles we are destined to play and some of us can spend a lifetime looking for the person we should have been from the very beginning. Some tomboys simply are what they have to be, and some are like me — lost souls flailing around in the confusion until eventually they find something they can hang on to.

I have no idea what happened to the boy with the flagrant shins. I haven't seen him since high school graduation. He may have gone to Vietnam, or he may be living five miles down the road from my father — I don't know where he is.

Wherever he is, I hope his wounds have healed.

not too long ago a friend brought me an advertisement for a cat stroller.

I love to buy things, but it never occurred to me before that I might need a cat stroller. This particular stroller appears to retail for around $130. (It occurs to me I don't even know how much I should reasonably pay for a baby stroller.) The advertisement shows happy small dogs (and some foreign animal I don't recognize) all at home in their strollers. The strollers have open mesh areas, and fabric-enclosed areas for "privacy." It states that this stroller is "great for city dwellers who own cats or small dogs."

I own a cat. (Well, I share my home with a cat. Actual ownership is a question of attitude.)

I live in a city. (I live in an area where the houses are close together and it is against the law to shelter live-stock. If I were to show my city to someone from San Francisco or New York, they would probably look around and say, "Where?")

Other advantages to the cat stroller: it's not "hot" like plastic carriers; it can be used for hauling groceries as well. It folds up for easy storage.

I know that Babycakes would love a stroller.

Until I threw it away, he had taken up residence in a paper bag. I don't remember how the bag fell on the floor, but once it did it filled up with fine gold fur almost immediately, and whenever I would walk past the bag a small paw would snake out and snag my ankle. This was apparently a lovely way to pass the time, but his mani-curist moved to Mishawaka and my red blood cell count began to fall. Trim his nails/throw away the bag. Trim his nails . . . Unfortunately I had misplaced my asbestos gloves, so I threw away the bag.

(I should be honest here. His manicurist is younger than I am. She is, in fact, exactly young enough to be my Beloved's Girlchild. When she trimmed his nails, she sat down on her knees on the floor and shoved large wads of cat through her crotch, hauling out only the paw she wanted to work on. As I watched her do this, several problems came immediately to mind: (a) the last time I sat comfortably on the floor on my knees I was less than twenty. They are not the same knees I have now; (b) if I stuffed a cat into my crotch while I was sitting on my knees on the floor, it would crush the cat; (c) I've seen what he's done to my *wrist* when he lost his temper. Once his manicurist moved, we struggled with slash wounds for a while, and finally I discovered I could slam him down on the waterbed, hold him down with one knee, and trim two to three nails per adventure until we were done. This is similar to a number of other bed games we play, and he has been known to purr through a claw-shortening.)

Unlike other cats I have lived with, Babycakes is not difficult to get into a carrier. Often all I need to do is set

the empty carrier on the floor with the door open—
someone with just slightly more patience than I have
could simply watch him walk inside. I often don't plan
my life well enough to wait for curiosity to overcome my
cat, and I grab him and shove him in. He does not
approve of this behavior but he tolerates it. He has been
known to take naps in stray carriers left sitting around. I
once lived with a four-pound princess who could attach
an appendage to every edge of the carrier and brace herself for dear life. By the time I had shoved her inside, the
tablecloth, everything on the table, and most of my shirt
were in there with her. The worst protest I have ever
received from Babycakes is an annoyed little "pfft,"
which means, *When my nails grow out again and you're sleeping, witch, your left ear is toast.* It's a dignity thing.

Babycakes does not mind riding in the truck. He
rarely talks, almost never cries or whines. Often he will
curl up and take a nap.

It would seem Babycakes would be the perfect cat
for a stroller. I could take him to parks, walk him around,
let people admire my beautiful house cat . . .

Not too long ago friends came to visit me. Altogether
there were three of them, all confirmed cat people, all
dedicated readers and admirers of Babycakes' contribu-
tions to the last book. They were excited to see him. I
brought them into the house. I picked him up, held him
firmly and supportively in my arms, and carried him
slowly and reassuringly to his adoring public.

They spoke to him warmly and lovingly.

One friend reached out to touch his soft and beautiful fur.

Babycakes laid his ears back, bared his teeth, and leaked compressed air like a punctured tire.

His admirer jumped back like a Bengal tiger had lunged at her.

I said, "What the . . . ?"

He looked at me and gave me that I-am-a-mysterious-being look of his.

At no time during this entire exchange did he even bother to stop purring.

I can see myself spending my new literary fortune on a cat stroller for my inspiration and cowriter. I could take him to book signings with me, and he could lounge in the private section when he became too tired, and come out to the mesh section when he chose to be admired. His public could ooh and aah at the wonderfulness of his fine gold self and every now and then, just to assure his place in literary society, he could threaten to rip someone's throat out.

It sounds like $130 well spent.

cheating death

There is a woman on television
who is wearing my mother's
cheekbones, and another
has stolen that certain gesture
that once identified her hands.
Memories are everywhere, always:
a passing scent, the swish of fabric
moving—dancing as she loved to dance.
The face in my mirror, my nephew's smile,
my sister's taste in shoes.
Dust to dust, ashes to ashes,
she filters down around me like
the late evening fog cuddles
a groggy field, like rain
soaks into the thirsty earth.
She is never here with me/
She is always here with me.

the kitten

not all memories are what they first appear to be. Some are little packets of time or place or experience that explain how the rememberer came to be the person they are. Some can be a series of elements tangled together with no distinct form or substance—a feeling, perhaps, like a small ache in the chest, with a few mental photographs and an odd smattering of autobiographical data that may or may not have anything to do with the event being remembered. And some are like pearls, bright, cheerful, obviously of value and oblivious to the fact that a pearl is an irritant endlessly polished until all of the sharp edges are smooth. If I had to name the memory I want to tell you about, I would call it "homesick," which is almost but not quite the right word. It's a memory about a kitten.

This is what I remember.

I wasn't very old. I don't know how old I was. I can only try to recall that event as clearly as I can, and tell you how the way I saw things then is different from the way I see them now.

I was me. No questions, no doubts, no blurring of the perimeters. I was me, and I was the only me there was or ever had been. Everyone around me mattered or did not depending on what they did or did not do for me. I acknowledged that they appeared to have lives that went on when I could no longer see them living, but these lives were not important.

My parents were perfect. My mother was beautiful and funny and just a little more alive than the other women. My father was quiet and strong and soft-spoken (unless you made him mad). I loved them. They loved me.

I had once been the center of their life, but that had changed. I had recently become a "Big Sister," as if this were a title of great honor and prestige, or indeed, as if I had asked for or done anything to help effect this change in my life. All of my parents' friends had come to see the baby, had cooed and aahed over the baby, had talked endlessly about and brought presents for the baby, and then they would turn to me and say, "*There* she is, the proud new Big Sister." I was not warming to sisterhood as quickly as everyone had hoped.

As a necessary bit of history for my story, my father brought home a kitten for my mother back when I was too small to remember. I was one, at the time. The kitten's name was Gus, and Gus was our family cat. My mother said Gus ran our house. Gus was an excellent cat and an exceptional mouser, but not a particularly satisfactory pet. When I tried to wrap her in baby blankets and feed her like my mother fed the new baby, Gus scratched me and stalked away. My mother would say, "There's not much I can do about that—she's a cat." Gus slept at the foot of my bed. Several times she had her kittens there while I watched. I was fascinated, my mother less than pleased.

Both of my parents had grown up on dairy farms. Neither of my parents wanted to farm themselves. Farming was never-ending, unrelenting work. "I don't want to be tied down to a herd of cows my entire life," my mother said. I understood this. Anytime we went anywhere with my grandparents, we had to be back in time for them to do the milking by 5 p.m., even if we liked where we were and we had been having fun doing what we did. Even if something even better to do was planned for later, we had to leave because they had to go home and feed and milk the cows.

The only things I liked when we helped to milk and feed the cows were the cats. I was young enough that my job, helping with the cows, was primarily to stay out of the way and in the less active places in the barn. There were always cats around the barn. Most of them were half-feral and half-starved, so I would only get to see them when someone poured them a bowl of milk. Their hunger would temporarily overrule their fear. But there would be friendly cats as well, cats I could pet. Kittens to find in their burrows in the haymows. There were always kittens. The life of a barn cat was often short, but remarkably fertile.

Gus had probably been a barn kitten. Some farmer gave her to my father. She had apparently not enjoyed the communal life all that much, because after she came to live with us, she drove off every cat and dog in the neighborhood, often including her own children. And she was a pet, which is one step up from a barn cat, but in those days when money was tight and the farm across the road still smelled like manure in the spring and hay in the late summer, it was not a big step. My parents did not spend "good money" on vet bills. They never had her spayed. She presented them with two to three litters of kittens a year, six kittens to the litter, for a good ten years. We were not allowed to bring the kittens in the house—only Gus could come in the house. The kittens lived outside, where they were hit by cars, or hunted by coons or dogs or who knows what else, and where their expected life span was a little over six months.

No one I knew treated their pets any differently than we treated ours. We were normal.

My mother liked cats. I took the care and welfare of my kittens very seriously, naming each and every one of them, and I found them when Gus hid them from me and I handled them every day. But my mother would sometimes come out and look at them with me and play with them for a while. She was always quick to pick up on their personalities, and she loved to tell funny stories about things the kittens did. Our cats loved her.

I don't have any memory of what the occasion was. Some friends of my parents had come over to our house. We probably had a big potluck picnic in the yard. There was a big, largely unused gravel pit behind our house, and in the pit there was a big pond, and for some reason my parents hauled a rowboat down onto the pond and my dad rowed my mother around on the water. I presume they must have hauled down more than one boat, so their friends could enjoy themselves as well. What I remember is that all of the adults seemed to have a wonderful time.

One of the kittens—one of maybe a hundred kittens

in my childhood, a kitten my mother and I raised whose name I have long since forgotten—one of the kittens jumped into the water and swam behind my parents' boat, swimming for all he was worth, as if he could not bear to be on land while my mother was out there on that godforsaken water. Wherever they rowed, he followed them, swimming madly, as if his life depended on his ability to keep up with her.

My father had a mean streak. Not a mean streak, really—a little-boy streak, let's say. A little wayward bent of mischief that could overpower his better judgment sometimes. He may have deliberately rowed the boat farther than he had intended, just to see how far the kitten would swim.

Do I remember the kitten? He wasn't very old, as I remember, maybe two or three months. In my mental picture he is a dark gray tiger, but then, in my mental picture—which may or may not be real—he is wet. The voice that directs me through the corridors of memory keeps telling me, *It doesn't matter about the cat—it's not about the cat.* But if I take away the cat, there is no story.

In my mental images I am standing above them all on a high bank overlooking the pond. I am not allowed to join them or go down into the gravel pit where they are because the pit is "dangerous." I can see my father with his mischievous grin, rowing the boat along just ahead of the kitten while my mother protests, "Bob . . ." It's not clear to me whether she wants him to stop, or if her protests are just part of the game. She is laughing. All of the adults are laughing, having a good time.

It seems so simple to me from where I am standing

above them. My mother should stop the boat and pick up the kitten. Hold him in her lap for a while. He so obviously loves her, it is perplexing to me that she cannot see it—or that it seems not to make any difference to her if she can. It makes my chest hurt, standing there up above them, to watch how hard he is willing to work just to be with her and how little it matters to her that he does.

Floating in my mind, disconnected from this memory apparently, just lost in the halls of childhood memory is a question. *Just what* would *it take to impress you?*

My mother may have stopped the boat. I don't remember. She may have.

A day or so later the kitten died, my mother said, of exhaustion and probably pneumonia.

I had easily a hundred cats in my life, when I was a child. I can tell a lot of cat stories, many with more details certainly than this one. I don't know why it's stuck so stubbornly in my mind all these years, just a story about a silly kitten that wanted to be with my mother so much he killed himself trying to reach her, and she thought it was funny.

tyger, tyger, burning bright

as i think this through it is just about two weeks after the amazing Las Vegas act of Siegfried and Roy came to an unpleasant end. A performing tiger grasped Roy by the throat and towed him backstage for a timeout. Many people are amazed that this kind of thing could happen to a man who worked with big cats all of his life (well, two people are amazed), while others are just amazed he's still alive. Neither amazes me, particularly. I live with a tiger. What amazes me is that the man worked and lived with tigers for thirty years and apparently he was allowed to sleep.

My tiger weighs twelve pounds. He doesn't know this, of course: if you were to introduce him to one of Siegfried and Roy's six-hundred-pound cats, he would fluff up his ruff and growl and lash his tail as if he were annoyed by the trespasses of another animal so obviously too stupid to live. He would give the interloper the opportunity to flee, not because the notion of combat concerned him, but because that is what tigers do. And because he is not completely stupid, if the interloper refused to leave, my tiger might walk over to sit under a low-lying chair and issue endless strings of threats and foul consequences, but he would not run. On a trip to the vet once he hissed at my truck, which weighs considerably more than a white tiger.

Roy is alive because his tiger was vexed; there is no doubt in my mind. If the tiger had wanted him dead, he would be dead. The problem Roy ran into—that all of us who live with tigers run into—is that vexing a tiger is neither difficult nor a notably slow process. My tiger, for instance, can go from dead asleep to vexed in a millisecond. I can be sleeping peacefully in my bed, flop out a hand and accidentally strike my sleeping tiger, and find him wrapped around my hand like an inverse porcupine, all twenty claws burrowing for bone, all four hundred teeth just locked around my wrist, gnawing for my jugular.

I have my own professional opinion of what happened between Roy and Montecore onstage that day. I wasn't there, I didn't see it, but any number of opinions have been offered with equally impressive qualifications and this is mine.

Montecore was having a bad day.

Montecore said to himself, "Enough of this puny little twit who can't even hunt for himself—I'm taking over the pride."

He said to himself, "I'll just grab him gently by the throat and drag him over to the side and explain the new rules to him. He's not a bad man—he feeds me—he just needs a little training."

When your tiger weighs twelve pounds and he decides to take command of the house you simply say, "Excuse me?" and he wanders off to take a bath and smooth out the kinks in his coat. When your tiger weighs six hundred pounds and he decides to take command of the house, you may not get the chance to say anything.

Perhaps Roy was just overtired that day.

I suggest this because I too live with a mobile alarm clock. I woke up this morning (one of the many times I woke up this morning) when twelve pounds of tiger jumped off the headboard and landed on my belly. I woke up when he burrowed under my blankets and affectionately kneaded my left ear with his claw. I woke up this morning when he settled in beside me, belly to belly, and retracted all twenty of his nails, which were still embedded, like tiny journalists, in my soft and comforting flesh.

I gave up that whole silly notion of sleeping in eventually because I had to go to the medicine cabinet and stanch the bleeding anyway, but as I did so I imagined this scene in my mind. Roy is in bed. Asleep. He stayed out late the night before—much the way I did—and now he is trying to make up his sleep. One of the many tigers who live in his house comes galloping through in a rip-tear (which all cats are prey to), skids to a stop on the carpet, and thinks, *Oh my God—it's morning and he's still asleep.*

I'll just climb up on this headboard here and bounce on his chest.

I will wake him gently as I wake my fellow tigers by lying belly to belly next to him and gently kneading his pathetic fur with my claws. This is a sign of intense affection among tigers. This is why all cats have seven different kinds of hair layered in their coats—to survive the affections of their peers.

Look at that foolish man, he has accidentally buried his head under his blankets. I will just burrow in and gently wash his ear with my tongue. I have never been washed with a tiger tongue, but if my own tiny tiger is any gauge it must be like being scraped with stainless steel Velcro.

Why do you put up with this? my friends ask me — as I am sure they ask Roy. I expect the question makes about equal sense to us. Because they are cats. Because that is the way cats are. Because part of living with anything is respecting those qualities that make it unique and define what it is. It does not surprise me in the least that while they wheeled Roy out on a stretcher, his greatest concern was that they not hurt his cat.

The cat did nothing wrong.

The cat was just being a cat.

That particular cat weighed six hundred pounds, but what he did is not remarkably different from what my twelve-pound companion, so aptly named "Babycakes," might have done in the same situation.

Cats are cats. Dogs are dogs. Grizzly bears are grizzly bears. I suspect the bear expert who was just recently mauled to death by his expertise would say the same thing: we can choose to see an animal however we like, but what we want to see will not change their nature. Their own rules for behavior are instinctual, immutable, and effective. They work.

Roy Horn understood the risk and he willingly took it and thirty years later he was badly hurt. I am sorry for his injury. I am sorry about the man who was mauled to death in Alaska by bears.

As I sit here writing, my cat, who has worked so hard to get me up, has migrated up into my lap and then into my arms, where, his heart beating against mine, he has settled into a nap. He sees no irony in this, and for him, there is none.

insurance

when i was about nine years old I ran over to our telephone to call my best friend and share some amazing
piece of information with her and when I picked up the
receiver she started talking to me. I had never dialed her
number. The phone had never rung. Astounded by this
undeniable evidence, I determined that I had extrasen-
sory perception and I was destined to grow up to locate
dead bodies for the FBI. Inevitably some would doubt
me, but I would become legendary for my gift, which I
decided, right there on the spot, would be finding missing children.

That was forty-five years ago and so far exactly no
missing children have reported their whereabouts to me,
but I was young then, and I did not yet understand how
quickly dreams can wither and die.

I shared my dream with my father's mother, who told
me she too was blessed with the Gift. She gave me several examples of her talent, all of which caused my eyebrows to furrow and my eyes themselves to flit nervously
over to my mother. I wanted to become rich and famous
for doing good (effortlessly, if at all possible). I had not
anticipated that seeing the ghost of some several-days-
dead neighbor might come as part of that package. I was

willing to *find* dead people — I was not particularly anxious to talk to them, or watch them wandering around my house.

My grandmother also told me that the elder of my two aunts had been born with a caul, which, never having heard before, I mistook for "towel" and had some difficulty piecing together into a seamless narrative.

Since I so obviously came from a family of seers, I practiced ESP religiously every day, my nine-year-old gifted self seizing, just moments after it happened, the intuition that exactly that event was going to happen minutes ago. I stared intently at the backs of playing cards. About the only real skill I ever demonstrated in ESP was hearing footsteps behind me — particularly if I happened to be walking at night — and imagining the more and more grotesque and horrible ghosts who made them. The day my mother came home from an evening out and found me and all of the smaller brothers and sisters under my charge quivering in terror behind our couch she suggested a career change. "There will be no more ghosts in this house," my mother decreed, and beyond the odd wind that slammed doors on occasion, the house ghosts were pretty much limited to those who hid behind the doors I had to walk through to turn on lights.

Bitter, disillusioned, I perceived that I actually had no ESP at all, that I had simply picked up a telephone once by sheer fluke, and I would need something more substantial than that to support me when I got old. Which, at that time, meant seventeen or eighteen.

Had I stayed in the small town where I grew up and

within the socioeconomic community in which I was born, that would doubtless have been the end of my story. I would have gotten married. According to the Ouija board, I would have had five children, all boys, and raised horses in Montana. The fact that I was not particularly enamored with children or horses probably did not seriously affect my Ouija future, but the fact that I was not particularly enamored with men brought that whole marriage scenario to a dead stop.

I became a feminist.

A week later I became a lesbian feminist.

A year after that I cast off the yoke of my oppressive, unsupportive straight sisters and became a feminist lesbian.

I did all of this from a very quiet little closet not all that far from the house where I was born, but the important thing is that—spiritually—I *did* it.

I snuck out of town in the dead of night and ran without lights to small gatherings of lesbians, where I determined, in my own supportive and nonjudgmental way, that every last one of them was crazier than a loon.

They turned God into a woman. They claimed She had originally been one. They described their moods in terms of the movements of the planets, they told their fortunes with oversized playing cards, they thought in loose and loopy strands of logic like, "That must be what the Universe was trying to tell me."

They processed. Endlessly. There is no thought that can be expressed in English—no matter how vaguely— that a herd of lesbians will not sit down and immediately begin to process.

The problem for me, of course, was that in the egalitarian ethos of feminist lesbians, every opinion and every belief is of equal weight and validity as every other, so my traditional big-sister *My way is right, your way is wrong, so quit whining and do it my way* was not received all that positively by my spiritual sisters. *We have to* talk *about this*, they would protest, as if they had been doing anything else for the past three days.

The word "open" popped into any number of conversations that came up around me, as in *You have to be more open,* or *Can you be open to that?* It is exactly conversations like that that have caused me to at least try to seriously consider any number of stupid ideas.

Unfortunately, what I lacked in personal openness I could more than make up for with imagination. A week after I moved out of my mother's house and into a home of my own I went out and got myself a cat. I grew up with cats. They are darling little creatures who hunt in the dead of night, who leap out at you in dark hallways, who run like coked-up junkies across rooms and up walls and hit the floors again with loud thuds. When you are lying in bed all alone in an apartment of your very own it is comforting to know that the thumps and thuds and bangs and footsteps in the hall are all caused by the small, furry little creature you have chosen to share your home with. Even if that little creature is lying on your pillow, snoring loudly in your ear. I have always thought of my cats as insurance. If you pay enough food bills and litter bills and vet bills, the home invaders will go to someone else's house.

For fourteen years I lived in a house on Dettman

Road in Jackson, Michigan. The house was about sixty years old and perched on the side of a hill two and a half blocks from where it was originally built. It was moved, local natives were eager to fill me in, during a burst of civic industry some years before.

Where did you buy your house?

Oh yeah, I know that house — they moved that, you know, it used to be down in the hollow on Michigan Avenue where the Alano Club is now . . .

I lived with four cats on Dettman Road. I would curl up in my bed with one perched just above my head, one ignoring me from the foot of the bed, one folded like royalty in the arch of my hip, and one tucked up against my chest, and I would wake up to the odd impression that people were walking around my house, talking to themselves. I could hear their conversations: I could never make out any of the words. I never saw them. I blamed the phenomena on people outside the house, on the street or perhaps in the neighbors' yards. I would lie there in the dark and I would look at the cats, all sleeping peacefully and soundly around me, and I would promise myself that if there truly were invisible people walking around, talking inside my house, one of those cats would at least twitch.

I met my Beloved, who lived an hour-and-a-half drive from my house. I began to spend a lot of time on the road, driving to her house, driving back home . . .

Two of the cats died. I put the house up for sale, bought a new house halfway across the state, and the two surviving cats and I moved in. A year after we moved in, one of the two remaining cats died. I was left with Babycakes — the youngest — a motley red tabby who, in his then ten years of life, had never looked like his coat actually belongs to a cat. Part of the problem is that, while he has more than enough hair to coat the rugs, my pant legs, and anything he might lie down on, he does not have that dense, rabbit-fur coat that many longhairs have. On the upside, he does not mat. Like his human, he just never looks . . . groomed.

When I first moved into this house it was quiet and stately and curiously detached from street noise. About the only thing I could hear from the outside was car doors slamming. I hear a lot of car doors slamming. Eventually I began to wonder exactly how many car doors there are in my immediate neighborhood.

I remember thinking, *It's still better than people walking around, talking to each other all night.*

I was sitting home alone in my house one night when I remember thinking, *This house is probably fifty years older than the house on Dettman — it just seems odd that it* never *makes any noises . . .*

Who makes up these thoughts and sifts them through your brains like they were your own? I am not a stupid woman — I know better than to thumb my nose at the goddess of the unexplained . . .

———

In the fall some friends and I went to a psychic fair in Camp Chesterfield, Indiana. Psychics of every imaginable specialty had set up tables in the dining room and for a small fee we could pick and choose our imagined fortunes. There was even a psychic willing to "read" my pet, and the idea made me laugh out loud.

At the same time . . . Babycakes had been steadily losing weight since the death of his companion cat. They had never struck me as being particularly good friends, nor did he give any other indication he was grieving. He did not appear to be unhealthy. But I was becoming concerned. In the end, my curiosity won.

The pet psychic was a kind woman who obviously loved animals and who obviously believed in what she was doing. This did not necessarily mean I believed in her, but I tried to be open to the experience. We determined that cats (even psychically) are "very secretive" about their health, but that he (a) was beginning his final transition, (b) had some sort of systemic disorder that prevented him from eating properly, or (c) had a hairball.

Laughing about it later with my friends, I agreed she probably had it covered.

Babycakes met me at the door when I got home, which is not unusual. He seemed exceptionally pleased to see me and could hardly bring himself to leave my side the entire evening. When I went to bed, he was right there, singing and purring in my ear. I remember thinking, *Apparently he likes the idea that I had a spiritualist talk to him,* but pushed it aside. We have always had a sort of feast or famine relationship. When he was younger he would be aloof and fairly see-if-I-care about my gallivanting, but since he has become an only cat—or perhaps just an older one—he has become more forgiving, more willing to waive the penalty period so we can get directly to forgiveness.

After my visit with the psychic, he began steadily gaining weight.

He also became . . . flightier. Noises that he used to shrug off seemed to startle him into flight. I began to notice gradually that he often behaved as if there were someone/something else in the house.

I put this down to a writer's imagination.

About a week after my visit with the cat psychic I happened to be home in the early evening—something of a rarity—and it occurred to me that I had been gradually becoming aware of the fact that this house, which once seemed utterly silent and unmoving, has developed any number of odd thumps and thuds and . . . essentially the kind of unexplained phenomena that I've always kept cats around to excuse.

You're losing it, I reproved myself. *You're going to have the whole family hunkered down behind the couch again if you keep this up.*

Behind me—perhaps in the next room—there was a loud BANG! and someone said, "Boo!"

It startled me: I jumped, and then I sat there, wondering who was in the next room, reminding myself that it hadn't sounded exactly like "Boo" and that little voice in my head said, *They can't make it sound exactly like one person talking to another—there's a rule against that.*

And I realized belatedly that I had just imagined a ghost who said, "Boo!" *A spirit with a sense of humor, no less,* I admired . . .

And my cat—my insurance against unexplained entities—roared into the computer room at about a hundred miles an hour and came to a dead stop and stared at me.

His hair was all sticking straight up, his eyes were like saucers, and he stared at me with that eerie cat-stare . . .

"As you open up, more and more things like that will happen," my Beloved counseled me, and told me about adventures she had had in one of her own homes.

"If you smudge your house, that stuff will stop," another friend counseled me, referring to the ancient art of burning sage or another herb to cleanse one's space of spirits.

I spent some time wondering why smudging my house would repel spirits. I mean, what are the rules, exactly? And did I truly *want* to repel this spirit, or ghosts, or . . . whatever it may be? What I wanted was more specific than that: I wanted to *know*. Had I opened myself to something beyond the ordinary realm of see/hear/feel, or was I torturing myself with my own overactive imagination?

I was still pondering this in some obscure way when I went away for the weekend. We had a lovely time, took our time coming home, and as I walked into the house I realized I was a little curious about what my "spirit" might have in mind to surprise me with next. I felt fairly safe because these adventures were too small and happened too infrequently to keep me keyed up enough to really scare me. I was being "open" to whatever life had to offer.

I looked down at the loving cat at my feet, and I thought to myself, "God, he's a beautiful animal." And I stroked him . . .

And then I sat down and I looked at him.

Every hair on that cat was in perfect alignment with

every other hair. His ruff was spread out just the way I like it, his tail was fluffed, his coat was thick and neatly brushed. He looked clean and healthy and just exquisitely groomed.

I don't know who brushed out my normally tacky-looking cat. I can't swear he didn't groom himself. The noises have stopped, and I no longer have that sense of "otherness" in the house . . . And I have no idea what any of it means. Perhaps I never had any experience with a spirit—perhaps Babycakes had some sort of psychic experience with which he eventually came to terms, and I only saw the iceberg tips of this event.

I have always been curious about the paranormal. I have always wanted to *know*, one way or the other: is there a spirit world, and if so, is it accessible to those of us who live on this side of the door? But my mother's oldest daughter has always known one thing for sure — the problem with keeping the door open is you're never sure what might walk in.

CHERYL PECK: I was an imaginative (if not an overly motivated) child whose creative bent went largely unappreciated in the Midwest, where I was born and raised. We will probably never really know how many literary masterpieces were lost through my mother's insistence that I "come back down here to earth, where the rest of us are." I attended the University of Michigan, where I discovered diversity, social injustice, political activism, loud gay people, drugs, the counterculture, butt-kicking art fairs, and the women's movement. Terrified, I scurried back to the rural red-and-white-checked work ethic I had known and despised as a child. I have lived within the confines of my imagination for most of my life and I am relatively happy there. Recently I have begun releasing small personal works on the general public.

As always, I am contemplating writing a book about something more interesting than my own life.

five things i have learned in fifty years

1. The fact that it smells delicious does not guarantee it will taste good.
2. Kicking small boys in the shins as hard as I can will not make me feel better.
3. When you step on the brakes and they are "mushy"— even if they kick in a second later—park the car.
4. The small red indicator light on the dashboard that says OIL *should* say IF YOU CAN READ THIS I'M PROBABLY ALREADY DEAD.
5. If you are an imaginative child who makes up her own friends, you should not let your parents watch movies about ventriloquists whose dummies take over their lives. It never happens: but it will fire the latent imagination of a brooding parent in just so many different ways.

five things i am still learning

1. The fact that it smells delicious does not guarantee it will be good for me.
2. Kicking grown men in the shins as hard as I can will not always make me feel better.
3. The actual mechanical reason why stepping on a pedal inside the car will make the wheels stop turning may not be a concept I will memorize in this lifetime: sometimes it's enough to know that it will.
4. Even newer, better-engineered cars require those same old annoying fluid exchanges.
5. If you are an imaginative child who makes up her own friends, buy a computer. Sooner or later someone may pay you to print what you've created out of someone else's life and besides, writers are a little odd anyway.